W9-AWT-479

Faith and Power

BERNARD LEWIS

Faith and Power

 Religion and Politics in the Middle East

OXFORD
UNIVERSITY PRESS

2010

OXFORD
UNIVERSITY PRESS

Oxford University Press, Inc., publishes works that further
Oxford University's objective of excellence
in research, scholarship, and education.

Oxford   New York
Auckland   Cape Town   Dar es Salaam   Hong Kong   Karachi
Kuala Lumpur   Madrid   Melbourne   Mexico City   Nairobi
New Delhi   Shanghai   Taipei   Toronto

With offices in
Argentina   Austria   Brazil   Chile   Czech Republic   France   Greece
Guatemala   Hungary   Italy   Japan   Poland   Portugal   Singapore
South Korea   Switzerland   Thailand   Turkey   Ukraine   Vietnam

Published by Oxford University Press, Inc.
198 Madison Avenue, New York, NY 10016

www.oup.com

Oxford is a registered trademark of Oxford University Press

Library of Congress Cataloging-in-Publication Data
Lewis, Bernard, 1916–
Faith and Power: religion and politics in the Middle East /
Bernard Lewis.
   p. cm.
ISBN 978-0-19-514421-5
1. Islam–History   2. Islam–Relations.   3. East and West.
4. Middle East–Religion.   I. Title.
BP50.L48   2010
297.2'720956–dc22   2010000451

9 8 7 6 5 4 3 2 1

Printed in the United States of America
on acid-free paper

For Fouad Ajami
in appreciation of his scholarship,
friendship, and courage

Acknowledgments

My thanks are due to the editors and publishers of the various journals and volumes in which some of the chapters in this book were originally published.

I would also like to express my thanks to Susan Ferber and Jessica Ryan of the Oxford University Press; to my friend Buntzie Ellis Churchill; and once agian to my assistants Annamarie Cerminaro and Marci Laidler, who have all contributed in various ways to the preparation of this book.

Contents

Foreword

In a famous passage in the New Testament, Christians are enjoined to "render....unto Caesar the things which are Caesar's; and unto God the things that are God's" (Matthew 22:21). In these words, a principle was laid down, at the very beginning of Christianity, that became central to both Christian thought and practice and that is discernible throughout Christian history and all over Christendom. Always, there were two authorities, God and, symbolically, Caesar; dealing with different matters, exercising different jurisdictions; each with its own laws and its own courts for enforcing them; each with its own institutions and its own hierarchy for administering them.

These two different authorities are generally known in the Christian world as "church" and "state." In the long and varied history of Christendom, the two have always been there—sometimes in association, sometimes in conflict; sometimes one predominant, sometimes the other—but always two and not one. The doctrine of the separation of the two is now accepted, in practice and sometimes in law, in most if not all of the Christian or post-Christian world.

In Islam, until comparatively modern times, such a doctrine was not only nonexistent but would have been meaningless. One can separate two things; one can hardly separate one. For a Muslim in classical Islamic times, the mosque is a building—a place of worship and study. The word was not used in the Christian institutional sense, because there was no comparable institution—that is, until modern changes took place under Western influence and example. In classical Islam, church and state are one and the same. They are not separate or indeed separable institutions, and there is no way of cutting through the tangled web of human activities and the authorities that regulate them; allocating certain things to religion, others to politics; some to the state and some to a specifically religious authority. Such familiar pairs of words as *lay* and *ecclesiastical, sacred* and *profane, spiritual* and *temporal,* and the like have no equivalent in classical Arabic (except to a limited extent among Arabic-speaking Christians), since the dichotomy that they express, deeply rooted in Christendom, was unknown in Islam until comparatively modern times, when its introduction was the result of external influences. In recent years, these external influences have been attacked, discredited, and weakened, and the ideas that they brought, never accepted by more than a relatively small and alienated elite, have become even weaker. And as external influences weaken, there is an inevitable return to older, more deep-rooted perceptions.

The political differences between the three interrelated Middle Eastern religions, Islam, Christianity, and Judaism, are clearly expressed in the narratives that constitute the sacred foundation history of the three. Moses led his people out of bondage and through the wilderness but was not permitted to enter the Promised Land. Christ died on the cross, and his followers were a persecuted minority until centuries later they converted a Roman emperor and entered into a long and problematic relationship with the Roman and then other states.

Muhammad, the Prophet and founder of Islam, achieved worldly success during his lifetime, becoming the head of a state that was soon to grow into an empire.

As the Ayatollah Khomeini reminded us, the Prophet Muhammad founded not only a community but also a polity, a society, and a state of which he was the sovereign ruler. As such, he commanded armies, made war and peace, collected taxes, proclaimed and enforced the law, and did all those things a ruler normally does.

All this meant that from the very beginning of Islam, from the lifetime of its founder, in the formative memories that are the sacred, classical, and scriptural history of all Muslims, religion and the state are one and the same. This intimate connection between faith and power remained characteristic of Islam in contrast to the other two religions.

There are other historical differences. Christianity arose amid the fall of an empire. The rise of Christianity parallels the decline of Rome, and the church created its own structures to survive in that period. During the centuries when Christianity was a persecuted religion of the downtrodden, God was seen as subjecting His followers to suffering and tribulation to test and purify their faith. When Christianity finally became a state religion, Christians tried to take over and refashion the institutions and even the language of Rome to their own needs. For a large and significant group of Christians, Rome, not Nazareth or Jerusalem, became the center of Christendom; Latin, not Aramaic or Hebrew, its sacred language. Islam, in contrast, arose amid the birth of an empire and became the basis of a vast, prosperous, and flourishing realm, created under the aegis of the new faith, and expressed in the language of the new revelation— Arabic. Although for St. Augustine and other early Christian thinkers, the state was a lesser evil, for Muslims, the state—that is, of course, the Islamic state—was a necessity ordained by divine law to defend and promulgate God's faith and to maintain and enforce God's law. In this perception of the universe, God is seen as helping rather than testing the believers, as desiring their success in this world and manifesting His divine approval by victory and dominance.

There is a partial exception to this in the minority and opposition sects that arose within Islam. Among the Shi'a, one finds an almost Christian-style conception of suffering and passion. This, combined with Muslim triumphalism, sometimes produced an explosively powerful social force.

These perceptions from the early history of Islam still have important consequences at the present time, notably in their effect on the shaping and character of Muslim self-awareness. Perhaps the most important and far-reaching of these effects is that for most Muslims, Islam rather than anything else is the ultimate basis of identity, loyalty, and therefore authority. In most parts of the modern world, it is usual, at different times and for different purposes, for people to define themselves collectively in a number of ways—by country, by nation, by race, by class, or by language, as well as some other criteria. All of these have their place in Islamic self-perceptions as reflected in historical writings, and sometimes that place is even an important one. But overall they are seen as secondary. For most of the recorded history of most of the Muslim world, the primary and basic definition, both adoptive and ascriptive, is not country or nation, not race or class, but religion, and for Muslims, that of course means Islam. In their view, it is religion that marks the distinction between insider and outsider, between brother and stranger, and at times between friend and enemy. Other factors, other loyalties no doubt operate, at various times and in various places, but to become effective, they had to assume a religious or at least a sectarian form. Two examples may suffice to illustrate this point: the first is the report of a military mission sent by the Ottoman sultan to Vienna in the seventeenth century. The note reports that "when we arrived we were welcomed by a group of five infidel officers who escorted us into the city." He means, of course, Austrian officers, but that is not what he says. The second example comes simply from a reading of nineteenth-century newspapers in Istanbul: "There was an accident on the bridge, and one unbeliever was injured." Both illustrate, in different ways, how religion was perceived as the ultimate basis of identity.

A striking example of the difference between Muslim perceptions of identity and loyalty and those of other religions can be seen in the conduct of international relations. The heads of state or ministers of foreign affairs of Christendom do not forgather in Christian summit conferences, nor does any group of them hold meetings on the basis of their current or previous adherence to one or another church. Similarly, the Buddhist states of East and Southeast Asia do not constitute a Buddhist bloc at the United Nations, nor for that matter in any other of their political activities. The very idea of such a grouping, based on religion, may seem to some observers in the modern world as absurd or even comic. It is, however, neither absurd nor comic in relation to Islam. Fifty-seven governments—monarchies and republics, conservatives and radicals, exponents of a variety of doctrines— have built up an elaborate apparatus of international consultation and, on many issues, cooperation. The Organization of the Islamic Conference, with fifty-seven members, has just celebrated its sixtieth anniversary. This organization holds regular, high-level conferences, and despite differences of structure, ideology, and policy, its members have achieved some measure of agreement and common action.

A similar difference may be seen in internal politics. Here, too, the difference between the Islamic countries and the rest of the world, though less total, is still substantial. In countries that practice multiparty open democracy, there are political parties that call themselves Christian or Buddhist. These are, however, very few, and even for some of these, religious themes play little or no part in their appeals to the electorate. In most Islamic countries, in contrast, religion is an even more powerful factor in internal than in international affairs.

Since Islam is perceived as the main basis of identity, it necessarily constitutes the main claim to loyalty, to allegiance. In most Muslim societies, the essential test by which one distinguishes between loyalty and disloyalty is usually religion. What matters here is not so much religious belief or theological conviction, though these are not unimportant; what matters is communal loyalty. And since conformity is the outward sign of loyalty, it follows that heresy is disloyalty, and apostasy is treason. Despite the vast changes of the last century or two, Islam has clearly remained the most accepted form of consensus in Muslim countries; Muslim symbols and appeals are still the most effective for the mobilization of social forces, whether behind a government or against it.

Thus, along with identity and loyalty, authority, too, is determined by Islam. In most Western systems of political thought and practice, sovereignty comes by inheritance and tradition or, in more modern times, from the people. Dynastic succession was, of course, well established in the Islamic lands, as everywhere else in the world, and such dynasties as the caliphs of Baghdad and the Ottoman sultans played a major role in Muslim history. But succession was by some form of nomination or selection. Primogeniture—the right of succession of the eldest son of the ruler—was unknown in the Islamic lands until it was introduced from Europe in modern times. It is now widely practiced in Muslim countries, including some republics.

In the traditional Muslim view, however, the ultimate source of a ruler's authority is neither his predecessors nor the people, but God. And since God is the source of authority, it is He who delegates and empowers the head of state, He, too, who is the sole source of law and indeed of legislation. If the ruler is God's ruler and the law that he enforces is God's law, then obedience to him is a religious obligation, and disobedience is a sin as well as a crime, to be punished in the next world as well as in this one. If the ruler does not draw his power from God, he is a usurper; if the law he administers is not God's law, he is a tyrant. In such a situation, the duty of obedience lapses and is replaced by a duty—not merely a right—of disobedience.

Muslim jurists and theologians, over the centuries, produced a considerable literature discussing such questions as legitimacy and usurpation. How does a ruler become legitimate? When does he cease to be legitimate? In what circumstances does the subject have the right or rather, in Islamic terms, the duty to disobey him and ultimately to remove him? Islam has its own corpus of revolutionary ideologies, its own record and memory of revolutionary actions, which still have a powerful evocative appeal. Recent events in Iran and in some other countries have given these memories a new relevance.

For most of modern history—more than two centuries in some areas, shorter periods in others—the heartlands of Islam were subject to the influence, the dominance, and at times the direct rule of European imperial powers. During this period of European domination and therefore influence, there was a series of different Islamic responses: acceptance and imitation, rejection and revolt. It is surely significant that when there was a genuine popular outbreak involving the masses and going beyond a small educated elite, the movement expressed itself not in nationalist, not in patriotic, not in social or economic, but in Islamic terms. During the first major phase of European expansion into the Islamic lands in the nineteenth century, when the British Empire was absorbing the Muslim northwest of India, when the Russians were conquering the Caucasian lands, and when the French were invading North Africa, in all three places the most effective and persistent resistance was Islamic— organized by Islamic brotherhoods, led by Muslim religious leaders. The careers of Aḥmed Brelwi (d. 1831) in India, of

Shāmil (d. 1871) in Dagestan, and of 'Abd al-Qādir (d. 1883) in Algeria all express the markedly religious character of this first major resistance in the Islamic world to the advance of imperial Europe in all three places.

In due course, all three were crushed, and a period of acceptance and some measure of accommodation followed. Muslim subjects of the three major empires—the British, the French, and the Russian—began, despite some opposition, to learn the languages of their imperial masters and even to adopt some of their cultural patterns.

A second phase in Islamic resistance came toward the end of the nineteenth century, when for the first time we find the word *pan-Islam* used to denote an explicitly political movement aiming at a greater unity of the Islamic world against European encroachment and domination. Already at that time we see what became a characteristic feature of such movements—the distinction between two kinds, one state-sponsored and used mainly diplomatically, the other oppositional and sometimes with more than a tinge of social radicalism.

By the early twentieth century, the European empires seemed to be the leading powers in the world, and constitutional and parliamentary government was therefore seen increasingly as the formula for success. This perception, expressed in the constitutional revolutions in Iran and the Ottoman Empire in the early twentieth century, was reinforced by the victory of the Western powers, the main standard-bearers of this form of government, in 1918. For a while, there were some stirrings of a new Islamic militancy, but with the consolidation of the secular Kemalist republic in Turkey and of the Soviet Union in Transcaucasia and Central Asia, this phase of Islamic activity ended, and a period of secular movements began—in some areas nationalist, in others socialist, in many both at the same time.

By the late thirties, this process was under attack, and the first stirrings of a new kind of militant Islam could be discerned.

This process was apparently halted in the early fifties by powerful rulers, notably in Iran and in Egypt, which had been the main centers of militant Islamic activity. Though the Shah in Iran and President Nasser in Egypt differed in many significant respects, they seem to have agreed in seeing militant Islamism as a threat to the kind of regime each was trying to establish, and in using whatever means were feasible to keep it under control. In Iran, the Shah failed and was overthrown and replaced by a militant Islamic regime. In Egypt, Nasser's successor is still in power but is increasingly threatened by radical Islamic opposition forces.

Such forces are now active all over the Islamic world and beyond, targeting first those they see as apostates and traitors at home, and beyond them, the ultimate enemy—the world of the unbelievers.

The following studies deal with a number of different aspects of the relationship between religion and government in the Islamic world—not between church and state, but rather between faith and power.

Credits

1. "License to Kill," *Foreign Affairs*, Vol. 77, No. 6, November–December 1998, pp. 14–19.
2. "Europe and Islam."—This was a paper delivered to a symposium held in Castelgandolfo, by invitation of the Pope, in 1987. The proceedings were published in German under the title *Europa und die Folgen*, edited by Krzystof Michalski, published in Stuttgart, Klett-Cotta, 1988.
3. "Religion and Politics in Islam and Judaism," Published in Hebrew translation in a volume of miscellaneous essays, *Ah'eret (Otherwise)*, edited by Aharon Amir, Guy Ma'ayan, Amir Or, Jerusalem, 2002.
4. "Islam and Liberal Democracy," *Atlantic Monthly*, February 1993, pp. 89–98.
5. "Free At Last? The Arab World in the Twenty-First Century," *Foreign Affairs* March–April 2009, pp. 77–88.
6. "Gender and the Clash of Civilizations." This is based on two lectures; one delivered at the University of Lucca, in Italy, on 17 December 2005; the other at the University of Tel Aviv in 2003. The lectures differ, but overlap. Neither has been published in the original English. A Hebrew

translation of the Tel Aviv lecture, based on a transcript, was included in a Hebrew volume on women in the Middle East, edited by Ofra Bengio, and published in Tel Aviv in 2004. The article included in this volume is based on the two lectures, but with extensive changes and revisions.

7. "Propaganda in the Middle East." A first brief sketch on this topic was published by the Hebrew University of Jerusalem, Faculty of Humanities, in their series *Jerusalem Studies in Arabic and Islam*, Vol. 25 (2001), pp. 1–14, and was reprinted in *From Babel to Dragomans: Interpreting the Middle East*, Oxford University Press, New York, 2004, pp. 97–113. Most of the study included in this volume is new and unpublished.

8. "Democracy and Religion in the Middle East." This was originally a paper presented to a conference held in Vienna on 3 July 1997 and published in German translation in the review *Transit*, Winter issue 1997. A Hebrew translation was published in the journal *Keshet* in the fall of 2004. Published in English in the Bassam Tibi *Festschrift*.

9. "Peace and Freedom in the Middle East." Unpublished.

10. "Democracy, Legitimacy, and Succession in the Middle East." This was part of a symposium held under the auspices of the Fondazione Magna Carta in Rome and published by them in a small book, *La Rivoluzione democratica contro il terrorismo*, edited by Fiamma Nirenstein, Mondadori, Rome, 2005.

11. "Freedom and Justice in Islam." This was a lecture delivered on 16 July 2006 to Hillsdale College and published by them in *Imprimis*, Vol. 35, No. 9, September 2006.

12. "Europe and Islam," American Enterprise Institute for Public Policy Research 2007 Irving Kristol Lecture, delivered 7 March 2007, and published as a booklet later in the same year.

13. "Freedom and Justice in the Modern Middle East," *Foreign Affairs*, Vol. 84, Number 3, May–June 2005, pp. 36–51.

Faith and Power

ONE

License to Kill

Osama bin Ladin's Declaration of Jihad

N FEBRUARY 23, 1998, *AL-QUDS AL-'ARABĪ*, AN Arabic newspaper published in London, printed the full text of a "Declaration of the World Islamic Front for Jihad against the Jews and the Crusaders." According to the paper, the statement was faxed to them under the signatures of Osama bin Ladin, the Saudi financier blamed by the United States for masterminding the August bombings of its embassies in East Africa, and the leaders of militant Islamist groups in Egypt, Pakistan, and Bangladesh. The statement—a magnificent piece of eloquent, at times even poetic Arabic prose—reveals a version of history that most Westerners will find unfamiliar. Bin Ladin's grievances are not quite what many would expect.

The declaration begins with an exordium quoting the more militant passages in the Qur'ān and the sayings of the Prophet Muhammad, then continues:

> Since God laid down the Arabian peninsula, created its desert, and surrounded it with its seas, no calamity has ever befallen it like these Crusader hosts that have spread in it like locusts, crowding its soil, eating its fruits, and destroying its verdure; and this at a time when the nations contend against the Muslims like diners jostling around a bowl of food.

The statement goes on to talk of the need to understand the situation and act to rectify it. The facts, it says, are known to everyone and fall under three main headings:

First—For more than seven years the United States is occupying the lands of Islam in the holiest of its territories, Arabia, plundering its riches, overwhelming its rulers, humiliating its people, threatening its neighbors, and using its bases in the peninsula as a spearhead to fight against the neighboring Islamic peoples.

Though some in the past have disputed the true nature of this occupation, the people of Arabia in their entirety have now recognized it.

There is no better proof of this than the continuing American aggression against the Iraqi people, launched from Arabia despite its rulers, who all oppose the use of their territories for this purpose but are subjugated.

Second—Despite the immense destruction inflicted on the Iraqi people at the hands of the Crusader-Jewish alliance and in spite of the appalling number of dead, exceeding a million, the Americans nevertheless, in spite of all this, are trying once more to repeat this dreadful slaughter. It seems that the long blockade following after a fierce war, the dismemberment and the destruction are not enough for them. So they come again today to destroy what remains of this people and to humiliate their Muslim neighbors.

Third—While the purposes of the Americans in these wars are religious and economic, they also serve the petty state of the Jews, to divert attention from their occupation of Jerusalem and their killing of Muslims in it.

There is no better proof of all this than their eagerness to destroy Iraq, the strongest of the neighboring Arab states, and their attempt to dismember all the states of the region, such as Iraq and Saudi Arabia and Egypt and Sudan, into petty states, whose division and weakness would ensure the survival of Israel and the continuation of the calamitous Crusader occupation of the lands of Arabia.

These crimes, the statement declares, amount to "a clear declaration of war by the Americans against God, his Prophet, and the Muslims." In such a situation, the declaration says, the ulema—authorities on theology and Islamic law, or *sharī'a*—throughout the centuries unanimously ruled that when enemies attack the Muslim lands, jihad becomes every Muslim's personal duty.

In the technical language of the ulema, religious duties may be collective, to be discharged by the community as a whole, or personal, incumbent on every individual Muslim. In an offensive war, the religious duty of jihad is collective and may be discharged by volunteers and professionals. When the Muslim community is defending itself, however, jihad becomes an individual obligation.

After quoting various Muslim authorities, the signatories then proceed to the final and most important part of their declaration, the fatwa, or ruling. It holds that

> To kill Americans and their allies, both civil and military, is an individual duty of every Muslim who is able, in any country where this is possible, until the Aqsa Mosque [in Jerusalem] and the Haram Mosque [in Mecca] are freed from their grip and until their armies, shattered and broken-winged, depart from all the lands of Islam, incapable of threatening any Muslim.

After citing some further relevant Quranïc verses, the document continues:

> By God's leave, we call on every Muslim who believes in God and hopes for reward to obey God's command to kill the Americans and plunder their possessions wherever he finds them and whenever he can. Likewise we call on the Muslim ulema and leaders and youth and soldiers to launch attacks against the armies

of the American devils and against those who are allied with
them from among the helpers of Satan.

The declaration and fatwa conclude with a series of further
quotations from Muslim scripture.

INFIDELS

Bin Ladin's view of the Gulf War as American aggression against
Iraq may seem a little odd, but it is widely—though by no means
universally—accepted in the Islamic world. For holy warriors of
any faith, the faithful are always right and the infidels always
wrong, whoever the protagonists and whatever the circumstances
of their encounter.

The three areas of grievance listed in the declaration—Arabia,
Iraq, and Jerusalem—will be familiar to observers of the Middle
Eastern scene. What may be less familiar is the sequence and
emphasis. For Muslims, as we in the West sometimes tend to
forget but those familiar with Islamic history and literature know,
the holy land par excellence is Arabia—Mecca, where the Prophet
was born; Medina, where he established the first Muslim state;
and the Hijaz, whose people were the first to rally to the new
faith and become its standard-bearers. Muhammad lived and died
in Arabia, as did the Rāshidūn caliphs, his immediate successors
at the head of the Islamic community. Thereafter, except for a
brief interlude in Syria, the center of the Islamic world and the
scene of its major achievements was Iraq, the seat of the caliphate
for half a millennium. For Muslims, no piece of land once added
to the realm of Islam can ever be finally renounced, but none
compares in significance with Arabia and Iraq.

Of these two, Arabia is by far the more important. The classical Arabic historians tell us that in the year 20 after the *hijra*
(Muhammad's move from Mecca to Medina), corresponding to
641 of the Christian calendar, the Caliph Umar decreed that

Jews and Christians should be removed from Arabia to fulfill an injunction the Prophet uttered on his deathbed: "Let there not be two religions in Arabia." The people in question were the Jews of the oasis of Khaybar in the north and the Christians of Najrān in the south. Both were ancient and deep-rooted communities, Arab in their speech, culture, and way of life, differing from their neighbors only in their faith.

The saying attributed to the Prophet was impugned by some earlier Islamic authorities. But it was generally accepted as authentic, and Umar put it into effect. The expulsion of religious minorities is extremely rare in Islamic history—unlike medieval Christendom, where evictions of Jews and (after the reconquest of Spain) Muslims were normal and frequent. Compared with European expulsions, Umar's decree was both limited and compassionate. It did not include southern and southeastern Arabia, which were not seen as part of Islam's holy land. And unlike the Jews and Muslims driven out of Spain and other European countries to find what refuge they could elsewhere, the Jews and Christians of Arabia were resettled on lands assigned to them—the Jews in Syria and Palestine, the Christians in Iraq. The process was also gradual rather than sudden, and there are reports of Jews and Christians remaining in Khaybar and Najrān for some time after Umar's edict.

But the decree was final and irreversible, and from then until now the holy land of the Hijaz has been forbidden territory for non-Muslims. According to the Ḥanbalī school of Islamic jurisprudence, accepted by both the Saudis and the declaration's signatories, for a non-Muslim even to set foot on the sacred soil is a major offense. In the rest of the kingdom, non-Muslims, while admitted as temporary visitors, were not permitted to establish residence or practice their religion.

The history of the Crusades provides a vivid example of the relative importance of Arabia and other places in Islamic perceptions. The Crusaders' capture of Jerusalem in 1099 was a triumph for Christendom and a disaster for the city's Jews. But to judge by the Arabic historiography of the period, it aroused scant interest in the region. Appeals for help by local Muslims to Damascus and Baghdad went unanswered, and the newly established Crusader principalities from Antioch to Jerusalem soon fitted into the game of Levantine politics, with cross-religious alliances forming a pattern of rivalries between and among Muslim and Christian princes.

The great counter-Crusade that ultimately drove the Crusaders into the sea did not begin until almost a century later. Its immediate cause was the activities of a freebooting Crusader leader, Reynald of Châtillon, who held the fortress of Kerak, in southern Jordan, between 1176 and 1187 and used it to launch a series of raids against Muslim caravans and commerce in the adjoining regions, including the Hijaz. Historians of the Crusades are probably right in saying that Reynald's motive was primarily economic—the desire for loot. But Muslims saw his campaigns as a provocation, a challenge directed against Islam's holy places. In 1182, violating an agreement between the Crusader king of Jerusalem and the Muslim leader Saladin, Reynald attacked and looted Muslim caravans, including one of pilgrims bound for Mecca. Even more heinous, from a Muslim point of view, was his threat to Arabia and a memorable buccaneering expedition in the Red Sea, featuring attacks on Muslim shipping and the Hijaz ports that served Mecca and Medina. Outraged, Saladin proclaimed a jihad against the Crusaders.

Even in Christian Europe, Saladin was justly celebrated and admired for his chivalrous and generous treatment of his defeated enemies. His magnanimity did not extend to Reynald of Châtillon. The great Arab historian Ibn al-Athīr wrote, "Twice, [Saladin said,] I had made a vow to kill him if I had him in my hands; once when he tried to march on Mecca and Medina, and again when he treacherously captured the caravan." After Saladin's triumph, when many of the Crusader princes and chieftains were taken captive, he separated Reynald of Châtillon from the rest and beheaded him with his own hands. After the success of the jihad and the recapture of Jerusalem, Saladin and his successors seem to have lost interest in the city. In 1229, one of them even ceded Jerusalem to the Emperor Frederick II as part of a general compromise agreement between the Muslim ruler and the Crusaders. Jerusalem was retaken in 1244 after the Crusaders tried to make it a purely Christian city, then eventually became a minor provincial town. Widespread interest in Jerusalem was reawakened only in the nineteenth century, first by the European powers' quarrels over custody of the Christian holy places and then by new waves of Jewish immigration after 1882.

In Arabia, however, the next perceived infidel threat came in the eighteenth century with the consolidation of European power in South Asia and the reappearance of Christian ships off the shores of Arabia. The resulting sense of outrage was at least one of the elements in the religious revival inspired in Arabia by the puritanical Wahhabi movement and led by the House of Saud, the founders of the modern Saudi state. During the period of Anglo-French domination of the Middle East, the imperial powers ruled Iraq, Syria, Palestine, Egypt, and Sudan. They nibbled at the fringes of Arabia, in Aden and the trucial sheikh-doms of the Gulf, but were wise enough to have no military and minimal political involvement in the affairs of the peninsula.

Oil made that level of involvement totally inadequate, and a growing Western presence, predominantly American, began to transform every aspect of Arabian life. The Red Sea port of Jiddah had long served as a kind of religious quarantine area in which foreign diplomatic, consular, and commercial represen-tatives were allowed to live. The discovery and exploitation of oil—and the consequent growth of the Saudi capital, Riyadh, from small oasis town to major metropolis—brought a consid-erable influx of foreigners. Their presence, still seen by many as a desecration, planted the seeds for a growing mood of resentment.

As long as this foreign involvement was exclusively economic, and as long as the rewards were more than adequate to soothe every grievance, the alien presence could be borne. But in recent years both have changed. With the fall in oil prices and the rise in population and expenditure, the rewards are no longer adequate and the grievances have become more numerous and more vocal. Nor is the involvement limited to economic activities. The revolution in Iran and the wars of Saddam Hussein have added political and military dimensions to the foreign involvement and have lent some plausibility to the increasingly heard cries of "imperialism." Where their holy land is involved, many Muslims tend to define the struggle—and sometimes also the enemy—in religious terms, seeing the American troops sent to free Kuwait and save Saudi Arabia from Saddam Hussein as infidel invaders and occupiers. This perception is heightened by America's unquestioned primacy among the powers of the infidel world.

TRAVESTIES

To most Americans, the declaration is a travesty, a gross distortion of the nature and purpose of the American presence in Arabia. They should also know that for many—perhaps most—Muslims, the declaration is an equally grotesque travesty of the nature of Islam and even of its doctrine of jihad. The Qur'ān speaks of peace as well as of war. The hundreds of thousands of traditions and sayings attributed with varying reliability to the Prophet, interpreted in various ways by the ulema, offer a wide range of guidance. The militant and violent interpretation is one among many. The standard juristic treatises on *sharī'a* normally contain a chapter on jihad, understood in the military sense as regular warfare against infidels and apostates. But these treatises prescribe correct behavior and respect for the rules of war in such matters as the opening and termination of hostilities and the treatment of noncombatants and prisoners, not to speak of diplomatic envoys. The jurists also discuss—and sometimes differ on—the actual conduct of war. Some permit, some restrict, and some disapprove of the use of mangonels, poisoned arrows, and the poisoning of enemy water supplies—the missile and chemical warfare of the Middle Ages—out of concern for the indiscriminate casualties that these weapons inflict. At no point do the basic texts of Islam enjoin terrorism and murder. At no point do they even consider the random slaughter of uninvolved bystanders.

Nevertheless, some Muslims are ready to approve, and a few of them to apply, the declaration's extreme interpretation of their religion. Terrorism requires only a few. Obviously, the West must defend itself by whatever means will be effective. But in devising strategies to fight the terrorists, it would surely be useful to understand the forces that drive them.

TWO

Europe and Islam

IN THE LATE FIFTEENTH CENTURY, THE PEOPLES OF Europe embarked on a great movement of expansion that by the mid-twentieth century had brought the whole world, to a greater or lesser degree, into the orbit of European civilization. The expansion of Europe took place at both ends—from the west by sea, from the east by land. In some regions, this expansion led to the domination and to the assimilation or exclusion of primitive peoples, and to the settlement by West and East Europeans of what were seen as empty lands. In others, the expansion brought Europeans into contact and often into collision with ancient civilizations and powerful states. By the twentieth century, all but a few of these states had been defeated and subjugated, and their peoples and territories laid open to European political, cultural, and economic penetration. And even those few that managed to survive in a European-dominated world did so at the price of the large-scale adoption of European ways.

In the course of their expansion to Asia and Africa, the Europeans encountered three major civilizations, those of India, China, and Islam. While the heartlands of Islam were in the regions now known as the Middle East and North Africa, inhabited predominantly by Arabic-, Persian-, and Turkish-speaking

Muslims, there were also vast Muslim populations and numerous Muslim states in the Eurasian steppe, the Indian subcontinent, the peninsula and islands of Southeast Asia, and important parts of black Africa.

In the developing relationship between an expanding Europe and these three established Afro-Asian civilizations, there was an important difference between Islam and the other two. Before the voyages of discovery and the expansion, India and China had been remote from European horizons, half-legendary countries known only from fragmentary references in the scriptures and classics and from the occasional reports of intrepid travelers. Among Indians and Chinese, even less was known of Europe, the very name of which, and of its peoples, had no place in the historic and literary records of these civilizations.

In the Islamic world, too, the name of Europe was virtually unknown. It appears in a few early Arabic translations or adaptations of Greek geographical texts, but it did not become part of the accepted geographical and political usage of medieval Islam and did not pass into general use until the late nineteenth century, when European political and hence also intellectual dominance brought the general acceptance of European nomenclature.

But if the name of Europe was unknown, the reality it denoted was old and familiar. Unlike its neighbors and predecessors, the Islamic polity defined itself by a religion, as a society in which identity and allegiance were determined by the acceptance of a common faith. For medieval Muslims, the world was divided into two: the house of Islam, where the faith and law of Islam prevailed, and the rest of the world, known as the house of war, to which the faith and law of Islam would, in due time, be brought by the Muslims. From an early date, Muslims learned to distinguish between the societies to the east and to the south, whose leaders professed no recognizable revealed religion and whose people could be seen as teachable recruits to Islam, and the peoples to the north and to the west, who professed

Christianity. If the name Europe meant nothing, the name Christendom meant a great deal.

Christendom and Islam had been neighbors, and more often than not enemies, since the advent of Islam in the seventh century. Between the two, there was an old relationship and even—though rarely explicit in either medieval or modern times—certain basic affinities.

What, then, did Islam and Christendom have in common? This question may be answered in both moral terms, as a shared heritage, and in material terms, as a shared—or, rather, disputed—domain.

Christianity and Islam, with their common predecessor Judaism, were all born in the same region and shaped by many of the same influences. The two later religions were both heirs to the ancient civilizations of the Middle East and to what came after them. Both were profoundly affected by Judaic religion, Greek philosophy and science, and Roman government and law. Both shared a wide range of memories and beliefs concerning prophecy, revelation, and scripture. These affinities, expressed in theology and even language, created a possibility of disputation and thus also of dialogue that could not have arisen between either Christians or Muslims on the one hand and exponents of Eastern religions like Hinduism or Buddhism on the other. Christians and Muslims alike denounced each other as infidels—and in so doing expressed their common attitude to religion.

As well as the shared heritage, there was also a shared domain. The expansion of the Muslim faith and state in the seventh and eighth centuries was largely at the expense of Christendom. From the Empire of Persia, the advancing Muslims took Iraq, by then a predominantly Christian country; from the Christianized Roman Empire and some other Christian states, they took Syria, Palestine, Egypt, North Africa, the Iberian Peninsula, and Sicily. Nowadays we think of Spain and Portugal as part of Europe lost to Islam and then recovered—but in the

Levant and North Africa, Christianity was older and more deeply rooted than in southwestern Europe, and its loss, especially that of the Holy Land, was a far heavier blow to medieval Christendom. Later, the expansion of the Mongols into Eastern Europe, and their subsequent conversion to Islam, brought much of the East European landmass under Islamic control. And while the Islamized Tatars dominated Russia and the steppelands, their kinsmen, the Ottoman Turks, were driving through the Balkan Peninsula toward the very heart of Europe.

Christianity and Islam alike had some difficulty in admitting the existence of the other as a major religion, a rival faith and civilization with an alternate message to humankind. Both sides expressed this unwillingness by the practice of denoting the adversary with ethnic rather than religious names. Muslims referred to European Christians as Romans, Slavs, or Franks; Europeans spoke of Muslims as Saracens, Moors, Turks, or Tatars, depending on which group they had encountered. But each was keenly aware that the other possessed and offered another revelation and dispensation; both expressed this awareness with such epithets as unbeliever, infidel, *paynim*, and *kafir*.

In chronological sequence, Christianity is the earlier and Islam the later religion. This had important consequences for their mutual attitudes. Each saw itself as the final revelation of God's purpose for humanity. For the Christian, the Jew was a precursor and, as such, could be accorded a limited and precarious tolerance. His religion was authentic but corrupted and incomplete. The Muslim could see both Jews and Christians as precursors, with holy books deriving from authentic revelations, but incomplete and corrupted by their unworthy custodians and therefore superseded by the final and perfect revelation of Islam.

Here again there is an important contrast between the responses of Islam, on the one hand, and of India and China on the other to the European expansion. For Hindus, Buddhists,

Confucians, and others, Christian civilization was new and unknown; those who brought it, and the things they brought, could therefore be considered more or less on their merits. For Muslims, Christianity—and therefore by implication everything associated with it—was known, familiar, and discounted. What was true in Christianity was incorporated in Islam. What was not so incorporated was false.

On the Christian side, there was a similar difference in attitudes to the three major Asian civilizations, and for obvious reasons. Neither Indians nor Chinese had ever conquered Spain, captured Constantinople, or besieged Vienna. Neither Hindus nor Buddhists nor yet Confucians had ever dismissed the Christian gospels as corrupt and outdated and offered a later, better version of God's Word to replace them.

While Christians and Muslims may have had little respect or esteem for each other's religion, both were keenly aware of the dangers that threatened them from the hostile powers inspired by those religions. For a very long time, this meant, in practice, a threat by Islam to Europe. For most of the Middle Ages, Islam was seen as representing a mortal danger. Within little more than a century, Muslim armies had wrested the eastern and southern shores of the Mediterranean from Christendom; they had conquered Spain, Portugal, and part of Italy and were even invading France. In Eastern Europe, the invasions first of the Tatars and then of the Turks continued the Muslim threat into modern times.

It is nowadays fashionable to present the Crusades as the first Western exercise in aggressive imperialism into the Third World. This interpretation is anachronistic and indeed meaningless in the context of the time. Essentially, the advance of Christian arms in the eleventh century was an attempt to break the Muslim pincer grip on Europe and recover the lost lands of Christendom. The repulse of the Muslims in France, the recovery of Sicily, and the gradual reconquest of Spain were all part of the same movement, culminating in the arrival of the Crusaders in the Levant at the end of the eleventh century. Like Spain and Portugal, Syria and Palestine were old Christian lands, which it was a Christian duty to reconquer, the more so since the latter included the holy places of Christendom. Their conquest by Islam was still comparatively recent, and they still held large Christian populations.

The recovery of southern Europe proved permanent, and Europe itself was in a sense delimited by the reconquest. In the Levant, the Crusaders failed. They encountered a new wave of Muslim expansion, led this time not by Arabs but by Turks, who had already conquered the greater part of Greek Christian Anatolia, and who were soon to bring Turkish Islam into southeastern and—through the conquests of the Islamized, Turkicized Golden Horde—Eastern Europe. And this expansion in turn brought a further European response, in the rise of Muscovy and, centuries later, of the Christian peoples of the Balkans.

The great European expansion from the end of the fifteenth century, at both the eastern and western extremities of Europe, was in origin a continuation of this process of European self-liberation. The Spaniards and the Portuguese drove the Moors out of Iberia—and pursued them to Africa and beyond. The Russians drove the Tatars out of Muscovy—and pursued them far into Asia.

In the west, the Spaniards and the Portuguese were followed by the other maritime nations of Western Europe and later, to a lesser extent, by the landbound continentals. In Eastern Europe, the Russians had the field to themselves in their expansion eastward and southward to the Caspian, the Black Sea, and Central Asia. In time, Eastern, Western, and Central Europe all met in a new drive to the Middle Eastern heartlands, as the power of the Ottomans faltered, weakened and finally failed.

In the eighteenth and nineteenth centuries, it was no longer Europe that was caught in Muslim pincers, but the Islamic lands in the pincers of European expansion. From the north, the Russians advanced into the Turkish- and Persian-speaking Muslim lands between the Black Sea and Central Asia. From the south, the maritime powers, from their new bases in South Asia and southern Africa, approached via the Indian Ocean, the Persian Gulf, and the Red Sea. Farther west, the Spaniards, followed, later and with greater success, by the French and the Italians, invaded Muslim North Africa. By the early twentieth century, most of the Muslim world had been incorporated in the four great European empires of Russia, the Netherlands, Britain, and France. Even Turkey and Iran, the two Muslim empires that had managed to hold on to a precarious independence in the age of European domination, were deeply penetrated by European interests, institutions, and ideas at almost every level of their public and, increasingly, their private lives.

The rulers of the Islamic world, from an early stage, were conscious of this European advance and of the danger it presented in the political, military, and economic aspects. The Ottoman Empire, from the sixteenth century the leading power of the Islamic world, showed some though not great awareness of the Russian and Western European expansion into Asia, more especially after the incorporation into the Ottoman domain of Egypt, Syria, and later Iraq and the extension of Ottoman power to eastern waters. An Ottoman expedition was sent to India, and a smaller one as far away as Acheh in Sumatra. Ottoman officials in the sixteenth century examined plans for the opening of two canals, one through the Isthmus of Suez, to allow the movement of Ottoman fleets from the Mediterranean to the Red Sea and beyond, and the other linking the Don and Volga rivers, to permit the deployment of Ottoman naval power from the Black Sea to the Caspian.

Nothing came of any of these projects, and in general, there seems to have been no real sense of urgency. Nor indeed was this likely, as long as the Ottomans were confident of their own overwhelming superiority against a Christian Europe divided by religious, economic, and even dynastic struggles. Europeans might be sailing and trading in remote places beyond the oceans, but the Ottomans firmly controlled the crucial crossroads where Europe, Asia, and Africa met. Ottoman fleets dominated the eastern Mediterranean, where the Christian victory in the Battle of Lepanto was no more than a flash in the pan. Ottoman armies came and went freely in southeastern Europe. For a century and a half, a Turkish pasha governed in Buda, and Turkish armies twice besieged Vienna. There seemed little reason for the Ottomans to fear or take precautions against European power.

There was even less reason for them to fear the onslaught of European ideas. European Christians in the Middle Ages had been keenly aware of Islam as a rival world faith, which at times seemed to threaten the very survival of Christianity. Countless Christians had embraced Islam. Indeed, of the early recruits to Islam outside Arabia, very many, probably the majority, were converts from Christianity. For European Christendom, the danger of Islam was religious no less than military. European Christian scholars learned Arabic, translated the Quran and other texts, and studied Islamic doctrine, for a double purpose. The first task, urgent and immediate, was to protect Christians from conversion to Islam. The second, more remote, was to convert the Muslims to Christianity. In this study of Arabic and Islam, we may discern the beginnings of what later came to be known as Orientalism. Some centuries passed before European Christians realized that the first task was no longer necessary and the second had never been possible. And in the meantime, with the Renaissance, the revival of learning, and the emergence of a new philological scholarship, the study of Arabic was assimilated to that of Latin, Greek, and Hebrew—classical and scriptural languages—in the European universities, and Orientalism entered a new phase that has continued ever since.

To these movements, there were no parallels on the Islamic side. While Christian power might at times have been seen as a threat, Christian religion was not, and the very idea was an absurdity. How could a Muslim be attracted by an earlier, abrogated version of his own religion, and moreover one professed by subject peoples whom he had conquered and over whom he held sway? Some knowledge of Christian beliefs was preserved in earlier Islamic literature, but there was no desire or attempt to learn European languages and to find out what was happening in Europe. The only exceptions were weaponry and more generally military technology, notably firearms and naval construction, and in these the Turks showed both skill and alacrity in acquiring, mastering, and sometimes improving the latest European inventions.

Of European cultural and intellectual life, virtually nothing was known. The Renaissance, the Reformation, even the wars of religion that convulsed Europe in the sixteenth and seventeenth centuries, passed almost unnoticed among Christendom's Muslim neighbors. Of European literature and science, only a handful of books were translated, and most of these were treatises on medicine, geography, and especially cartography. The translators were neither Turks nor Muslims by origin. A few were converts to Islam, but most were Christian or Jewish subjects of the Turkish sultans. Even printing, introduced by Jewish refugees from Spain before the end of the fifteenth century and later adopted by Greek and Armenian Christians under Turkish rule, was permitted by the sultans only on the condition that the Jewish and Christian printers printed no books in the Arabic script.

A major change began during the last years of the seventeenth century, as a direct result of the Turkish retreat from Vienna. For the first time since the entry of their armies into Europe, the Turks had suffered a major defeat on the battlefield and were compelled to relinquish and later to cede extensive territories. Until then, only the periphery of the Islamic world had been affected—the Russians on the Caspian, the Dutch in Java, both of them very remote. The retreat from Vienna was a blow to the heart.

It was the first of a long series of defeats, which in the course of the eighteenth century, despite occasional rallies, brought a decisive change in the balance of power between Islam and Christendom. Especially painful were the Russian annexation of the Crimea in 1783 and the French occupation of Egypt in 1798. The Crimea was not the first territory lost by the Ottomans to a European enemy. But the previous lost lands, like Hungary, had been Christian provinces under Ottoman occupation, mostly of brief duration. The Crimea was old Muslim Turkish territory dating back to the thirteenth century, and its absorption by Russia was followed by that of the entire northern coast of the Black Sea. The French occupation of Egypt brought Western influence to the very center of the Middle East, almost within striking distance of the holiest places of Islam.

The debate began in Turkey after the first defeat and was renewed with every subsequent setback. It revolved about two questions—what is wrong, and how can it be put right. An extensive literature was devoted to this subject, in Turkish and then also in Arabic and Persian. At first, it was largely the work of government officials and military officers. Later, with the emergence of new literate elements who were neither servants of the state nor men of religion, the debate became general and public.

The early memorialists saw the problem in military terms. The Christian enemy had somehow managed to establish a transitory military superiority. To remedy this, it was necessary to identify the sources of this superiority and make the necessary changes in the Muslim forces so as to equal and once again surpass the previously despised enemy. But the remodeling of the armed forces, on land and sea, led much further than the first reformers had intended or imagined. The new armies needed new supplies, and these involved developments in trade and industry. They needed better communications, and this meant roads, ports, railways, and the telegraph. They needed a new infrastructure, and this required administrative reforms and training civil servants of a new kind. They needed better intelligence concerning the enemy, and in a time of weakness, when diplomacy had to supplant or at least supplement military power in the defense of the empire, this meant political as well as military information and a study of the policies, polities, laws, and institutions of Christendom, of a type without precedent in the past. Above all, they needed new officers, and this in turn led to a demand for science and education.

In the second half of the eighteenth century, there were already European instructors serving with the Turkish armed forces or teaching in newly created military and naval schools. From the early nineteenth century, students were sent from Turkey, Egypt, and Iran to Europe in ever increasing numbers. At first, they were mostly officer cadets. Later, they included future diplomats and officials, and finally students in every field of study. To benefit from foreign instruction, whether at home or abroad, Muslim students had to accept a situation in which they were being taught by infidel teachers. Even more, they were obliged to learn infidel languages, a new and radical departure requiring a basic change of attitude. Contrary to all previous experience or at least belief, the knowledge of infidel languages became first useful, then esteemed, and finally—in almost every walk of life—necessary. For a while, Italian, then for a long time French, then English and in some areas German became keys to success and status in government, education, commerce, and—as they came into being—the professions.

With the knowledge of European languages came a first acquaintance with the values and ideas expressed in those languages. Muslim students were ordered to learn French to follow courses of military instruction, but some of them found other reading matter more explosive and perhaps more destructive than anything in the officer school training manuals. A closer acquaintance with Europe brought to Muslim readers and visitors a keener awareness of their own weakness, poverty, and relative backwardness, and a desire to seek out and adopt the talisman that lay at the root of the wealth and power of the mysterious Occident. More and more, Muslim inquirers found the secret of Western greatness in the two most distinctive and alien features they had encountered—industry and freedom, the one achieved by technology, the other by laws. The answer, so it seemed to the cheerful optimists of the nineteenth century, was simple: for the one, schools and factories; for the other, constitutions and parliaments. And these in turn rested on European science and philosophy, access to which became easier as a result of other changes that had in the meantime taken place in Europe.

A decisive change in the Muslim attitude to European culture was made possible by the French Revolution—the first extensive movement of ideas in Europe that was in no sense Christian and that could even be presented as anti-Christian. This was indeed the line adopted by French spokesmen during their occupation of Egypt and later in propaganda conducted from their embassy in Istanbul. Secularism as such had no appeal for Muslims, but an ideology explicitly divorced from Christianity could be considered and perhaps even adopted by Muslims aspiring to master the new European technology and institutions. In the past, as a modern Turkish historian has aptly put it, the tide of European science had broken against the dikes of theology and jurisprudence. The enthusiastic and hopeful liberalism of the nineteenth century opened a sluice in the dike, through which first a trickle and then a flood of new ideas penetrated and then inundated the hitherto closed Islamic world.

In the course of the nineteenth century, increasing numbers of young Muslims from Turkey, Iran, and Egypt had the opportunity to visit or even reside in Europe and to observe the functioning of European society and institutions at closer quarters. They included students; diplomats, becoming more important as the Muslim states adopted the European practice of maintaining resident embassies; merchants; and from the mid-century, exiles, as the example of European liberalism began to produce a domestic political opposition in some of these countries.

The range and depth of European influence in the Islamic lands during the centuries of expansion varied enormously. In some remote areas, like the Arabian Peninsula or Afghanistan, the impact of Europe was minimal and hardly went beyond the adoption of European firearms, with which the whole process of Westernization first began. At the opposite extreme were those regions, such as French North Africa and Russian Transcaucasia and Central Asia, where Muslim countries were forcibly incorporated into a European empire and obliged to learn the language of their imperial masters and to accept the presence of European administrators and even colonists in their midst. In an intermediate position between the two extremes were those countries, notably the Persian and Ottoman empires, where Muslim rulers had managed, more because of European rivalries than because of their own defensive strength, to maintain a precarious independence, but where their way of life was fundamentally transformed under the impact of European economic, political, and cultural penetration. It was in these countries that radical Muslim Westernizers, like Sultan Mahmud II in Turkey and Muḥammad ʿAlī Pasha in Egypt, or in a later generation, Kemal Atatürk in Turkey and Reza Shah in Iran, made far more sweeping changes than were ever possible for imperial rulers. These tended to be more conservative, and certainly more cautious, in their dealings with entrenched Muslim interests and institutions.

Until the latter part of the eighteenth century, Muslims visited Europe only as soldiers, prisoners of war, or diplomats. Their own religion did not encourage them to go; the religion of their European hosts did not encourage them to come, still less to stay for any length of time. While European Christians enjoyed much greater freedom to travel to Muslim lands, and even to establish themselves there as residents, this brought very little contact with the Muslims, whether the elites or the general population. The European colonies for the most part lived a segregated existence, and their necessary contacts with Muslim authorities were, so to speak, cushioned by intermediaries and interpreters drawn from the native Christian and, to a much lesser extent, Jewish population.

The nineteenth century thus brought a radical transformation. Young Muslims traveled to Europe and stayed there for some years to study. Their knowledge of European languages opened the previously closed doors to European literature, science, and thought. The reintroduction of printing and the establishment of newspapers and magazines in Arabic, Persian, and Turkish brought several significant changes: the opportunity, for the first time, to follow events inside and outside the Islamic world; the emergence of a new and more flexible language, with the conceptual and lexical resources to discuss these developments; and, in many ways most significant of all, the emergence of a new figure—the journalist.

Together with the journalist came another newcomer, whose appearance was equally portentous—the lawyer. In an Islamic state, there is in principle no law other than the Shariʿa, the holy law of Islam. The reforms of the nineteenth century and the needs of commercial and other contacts with Europe led to the enactment of new laws, modeled on those of Europe—commercial, civil, criminal, and finally constitutional. In the traditional order, the only lawyers were the ulema, the doctors of the holy law, at once jurists and theologians. The secular lawyer, pleading in courts administering secular law, represented a new and influential element in society.

Education, too, in the old order, had been largely the preserve of the men of religion. This also was taken from them, as reforming and imperial rulers alike found it necessary to establish schools, and later colleges and universities, to teach modern skills and dispense modern knowledge. The new-style teacher, sometimes schoolmaster, sometimes professor, joined the journalist and the lawyer as an intellectual pillar of the new order.

With the new laws, there came also a new political system, expressed in the constitutional and parliamentary orders set up in one country after another. This political process, involving competition for the good will of the electorate, as well as of the sovereign, produced another new element—the politician. And he might be a journalist, a lawyer, or a teacher, as well as a member of one of the older governing elites.

The three pillars of traditional authority—the soldiers, the officials, and the men of religion—were all divided among themselves, and there were Westernizers and anti-Westernizers, sometimes in violent conflict, in all three groups. But in the nature of things, it was the officers who were the most consistent Westernizers and the strongest supporters of modernization. It was they, after all, who had encountered the problem, and the need for a solution, in the most brutal and direct form. And it was they who were the first to realize that change might well be a condition of survival. This idea was, however, by no means universally accepted, and the history of Muslim attitudes to the West and to Westernization shows a sequence, almost a cycle, of response, reaction, rejection, and return.

At the present time, the dominant attitude in most of the countries of the Islamic world toward the West is one of hostility—the explosion of a long stored-up resentment, after years of domination and humiliation at the hands of what is seen as an alien and infidel enemy. For the greater part of their history, Muslims had been accustomed to a position of supremacy and domination. During the formative centuries that conditioned their collective memories, Islam had advanced and unbelief retreated; Muslims had ruled, unbelievers had submitted, and the leaders of the infidels, both abroad and at home, had recognized the superiority of Islam and the supremacy of the Muslims. In the broad realms of the Islamic empires, the Christian populations had either embraced Islam or accepted a position of tolerated subordination. Even the unsubjugated Christians beyond the imperial frontiers were compelled to accept the reality of Muslim power. In peacetime, they came as supplicants, seeking, and usually receiving, permission to trade. In wartime, they were taught the lessons of Islamic superiority on the battlefield.

The expansion of Europe, leading first to the loss of the Islamic dominions in Europe and eventually to the European invasion even of the heartlands of Islam, had changed all this. In a succession of defeats and humiliations, the Muslim had lost on all sides. By defeat in battle, he had lost his supremacy in the world. By the penetration of European influence and the adoption of European ways, notably by the emancipation of his own non-Muslim subjects, he had lost his supremacy in his own country and city. With the European-inspired emancipation of women, even his supremacy in his own home was threatened.

The resulting resentments have been building up for a long time. The events of the second half of the twentieth century— the discrediting of the West after its two self-destructive world wars, the retreat of empire, the growth of Western self-doubt and self-criticism, and finally the new and powerful weapon placed in the hands of Muslims by the Western discovery and exploitation of oil and by the money oil gave them—brought these resentments to a head and provided the means and the opportunity to express them.

In principle, this hostility was directed against Eastern as well as against Western Europe, since both had invaded Islamic lands and disrupted Islamic societies. In practice, however, the hostility was more strongly felt and more explicitly directed against the Western world—first against Western Europe and then against those other lands beyond the oceans, which were seen, not unreasonably, as an extension of European civilization.

There are several reasons for this difference in the Islamic reactions against Eastern Europe and against Western Europe. One obvious reason is the difference in the continuing relationship. While Western influence remains, Western power has retreated, and the countries formerly under Western domination are now free—or rather those who rule them are free—to choose their own ways. The Islamic regions affected by the expansion of Eastern Europe are still so affected; indeed, at the present time, these are the only parts of the Islamic world still incorporated in a Europe-based political system. In these countries, therefore, the reaction has either not begun or, if it has begun, its expression is severely impeded.

Even in those parts of the Islamic world not directly controlled from Eastern Europe, there was a well-grounded recognition of proximate power and the proven willingness to use it. This recognition imposed respect or at least caution, particularly in groups and countries within reach of that power.

More important, however, than such reasons is the unquestionable fact that in the greater part of the Islamic world the effective source of change was, indeed, the Western world—not only by the intervention of Western powers but also, and at the present time far more, by the penetration of Western ideas and the imitation of Western institutions. These have reshaped Islamic society and, in the course of time, have given rise to the changes that are now causing so much distress and anger. Certainly, the most conspicuous outward signs of the crass materialism denounced by the Islamic revivalists—the flaunting indecency of cinema and television, the crude self-indulgence of the consumer society—are of unmistakably Western provenance. No one could accuse the Soviet East of either popular entertainment or spendthrift consumerism.

There are, of course, many specific problems causing friction between Middle Eastern and Western states, and each of these is of paramount concern to those directly involved. But increasingly, such concern is limited to those directly involved, while other parts of the Muslim world are preoccupied with their own specific problems. A vivid illustration of this was the remarkably limited response to such events as the Israeli invasion of Lebanon in 1982 or the American bombing of Tripoli in 1986. A few years earlier, these would have brought mass demonstrations of anger and outrage all over the Muslim world. This time, there was little more than perfunctory diplomatic protests.

Far more important than any of these specific issues and the hostility they arouse is an underlying generalized resentment, directed against the intrusive and disruptive forces that have shaken and riven Islamic society. This resentment has causes far deeper than this or that policy or action of this or that government. What confronts us is not a quarrel between governments but a clash of civilizations, with issues that can hardly be formulated, let alone discussed and resolved, at the level of intergovernmental negotiations. And in this clash, in this generalized mood of resentment, every difference is exaggerated, every quarrel exacerbated, and every problem—one may hope for the time being—is insoluble.

In this mood of revulsion against Western civilization, it is natural that hostility should be directed most strongly against those powers, or that power, seen as the leader of the West and less strongly against those seen as minor and weaker figures in the Western world. It is equally natural that some should turn, with hope and expectation, toward those seen as the strongest and most dangerous enemies of Western power and the Western way of life, in politics and strategy, economics and ideology. So it was in the 1930s and early 1940s; so again during the cold war.

There had been several such upsurges of hostility in the past, usually provoked by some significant advance of European power at Islamic expense. One such occurred in the 1830s and 1840s, when charismatic Muslim personalities emerged and led movements of armed resistance, ultimately unavailing, against the French conquest of Algeria, the Russian subjugation of the Caucasian peoples, and the British pacification of Sind. Another such movement extended from the 1860s to the 1880s, when the Muslim world reacted with horror to a new tide of European conquest, which brought the Russians to Samarkand and Bokhara, the French to Tunis, and the British to Cairo. Another came in the aftermath of the First World War, when the former Arab provinces of the Ottoman Empire were divided between the British and the French, and the former Muslim provinces of the Russian empire were, after an interlude of separate political existence, reincorporated in a new political system with its center in Moscow. Even the retreat of the Western empires after the Second World War aroused new hostilities, in the struggles for Algeria, Palestine, and Java, and the passions and bitterness to which these struggles gave rise.

At first sight, there seems no obvious reason for the present surge of anger. European political domination has long since ended, and while the one remaining European empire seems to advance rather than retreat, it is not primarily in that direction that hostile attention is turned. European economic control in the Muslim lands has also ended and has given way to a European dependence on Middle Eastern oil and markets. The major conflicts are now regional rather than international—Iraq versus Iran, Turkey versus Greece, Morocco versus Algeria, as well as the ethnic, sectarian, ideological, and social conflicts within many individual countries. Even the Arab struggle against Israel, which was once seen as the last outpost of European imperialism, has now become more and more a regional, even a local issue, in which the European powers have virtually no part, and the superpowers appear as cautious patrons and sponsors, rather than direct participants.

The principal political objectives set in the past have indeed been achieved, and it is not surprising that the classical nationalist movements of the kind that flourished in the nineteenth and early twentieth centuries have lost much of their attraction. In their place have come loyalties that might perhaps be more accurately described as patriotic rather than nationalistic, concerned primarily and often exclusively with the interests of the various individual states, rather than with larger and vaguer ethnic or cultural entities. And these states have been much more concerned with the shifting pattern of alliances and rivalries within the region than with the outside world. Pan-Arabism, pan-Turkism, and pan-Iranism, for the time being at least, are in abeyance, and it is the foreign policies of Turkey, Iran, Syria, Iraq, Egypt, and the rest that must now concern us. In this respect, the Arab states of the Middle East appear to have followed the pattern set by the various republics of Latin America after the ending of Spanish Empire and, centuries earlier, by the kingdoms of Europe.

But the yearning remains for some greater and older identity, for some larger community and loyalty transcending the petty sovereignties of the new states fashioned from the ruin of empires, some authority nobler than the increasingly disreputable and tyrannical governments that rule these states. To this need, Islam—not just a religion in the limited Western sense of the word, but a complete system of identity, loyalty, and authority— provides by far the most convincing and the most appealing answer. This appeal is greatly strengthened by the feeling, by now widespread in Islamic lands, of having been violated, humiliated, and forcibly changed by infidel and hostile forces from outside. At a time when the economies, societies, and polities of these countries are being subjected to severe strains, the call to abandon evil foreign ways and return to true Islam evokes a powerful response.

This response takes many forms, which it has become customary to lump together and designate, loosely and inaccurately, as Muslim fundamentalism. There are, in fact, many movements of Islamic revival and militancy, often differing quite considerably from one another. Some are old, some new; some are traditional and conservative, some radical and revolutionary. Some spring from the grass roots; some draw their strength from the sponsorship and financing of one or other Muslim government. Three governments are principally engaged in this work, those of Saudi Arabia, Libya and Iran, and they diverge greatly in their policies, purposes, and methods. All of them agree on the need to return to the pure, pristine Islam of the Prophet and his Companions; to restore the rule of the Holy Law; and to undo the changes wrought in the era of foreign rule or influence. And all of them, including the leaders of the Islamic revolution in Iran, reveal a certain ambivalence in defining the changes to be undone and the manner of their undoing.

In the realm of material things—the infrastructure, amenities, and services of the modern state and city, most of them initiated by past European rulers or concession-holders—there is clearly no desire to reverse or even deflect the process of modernization. Nor, indeed, are such things as airplanes and automobiles, telephones and television, tanks and artillery seen as Western or as related to the Western philosophies that preceded their invention.

More remarkably, there seems to be little desire to abolish the Western-style political systems that now exist in most Islamic countries—the constitutions and legislative assemblies, the systems of secular laws and law courts, even the patterns of political organization and identity. Of the forty-odd sovereign states that now exist in the Muslim world, only two, Turkey and Iran, were independent sovereign states in 1914. A few more—such as Morocco, Egypt, and Yemen—had been sovereign states in the past and had retained some form of autonomy under foreign rule. Most of the remainder were new, created from old imperial provinces or dependencies, with new frontiers, new political structures, and sometimes even new or reconditioned names. Iraq and Jordan were the names of medieval caliphal provinces, not coterminous with the present states bearing those names. Syria and Libya are names borrowed from Europe—derived, in that form, from Greco-Roman antiquity and introduced to the inhabitants of these countries, for the first time, by Europeans in the modern period. And yet, in spite of their novelty and their alien origins, the new states, under these names, are now solidly established in the sentiments and loyalties of their peoples, and all awareness of their alien origin seems to have disappeared. Even more striking is the case of Palestine, another Greco-Roman term brought back from Europe. Its history as the name of a separate political entity began and ended with the British mandate, and yet, without a state and without any historic memory of separate sovereignty or even identity, it has become the focus of a compelling political cause.

Along with the European-style constitutions and parliaments, which survive even in revolutionary Islamic Iran, and the European pattern of nationally defined sovereign states, there is still a general acceptance of the underlying European ideologies, especially of the concept of political nationhood, both with its topside of liberal patriotism, and its underside of ethnic chauvinism. An example of the latter is racially and theologically expressed anti-Semitism, a comparatively recent import from Europe to the world of Islam, where it has had a considerable impact. Two anti-Semitic classics, the fabricated *Protocols of the Elders of Zion* and Canon Rohling's *Talmud Jew*, are among the most widely translated and widely read productions of the European intellectual tradition in the present-day Arab world.

Perhaps the most powerful, persistent, and pervasive of Western intellectual influences is the cult of revolution. The history of Islam, like that of other societies, offers many examples of the overthrow of governments by rebellion or conspiracy, and a few of challenges to the whole social and political order by leaders who believe that it is their sacred duty to dethrone tyranny and install justice in its place. Islamic law and tradition lay down the limits of the obedience owed to the ruler, and discuss—albeit with due caution—the circumstances in which a ruler forfeits his claim to the allegiance of his subjects and may, or rather must, lawfully be replaced.

But the notion of revolution, as developed in Europe in sixteenth-century Holland, seventeenth-century England, and eighteenth-century France, was alien and new. The first self-styled revolutions in the Middle East occurred in Iran in 1905 and in Turkey in 1908. Since then, there have been many others, and at the present time, a majority of Islamic states are governed by regimes installed through the violent removal of their predecessors. In some, this was accomplished by a nationalist struggle against foreign rulers; in others, by military officers deposing the rulers in whose armies they served. In a very few, the change of regime resulted from profounder movements in society, with deeper causes and greater consequences than a simple replacement of the people at the top. All of these, however, with equal fervor, claim the title revolutionary, which by now has become the most widely accepted claim to legitimacy in government in the Islamic world.

All these various kinds of revolutionary regimes, as well as the surviving monarchies and traditional regimes, share the desire to preserve and utilize both the political apparatus and the economic benefits that modernization has placed at their disposal. What is resented is foreign control or exploitation of the economic machine, not the foreign origin of the machine itself. Here again, there seems to be no great awareness of any link between the machine and the civilization that produced it.

In cultural and social life, the penetration and acceptance of European ways has gone very far and persists in forms that even the militants and radicals either do not perceive or are willing to tolerate. The first to change were the traditional arts. Already by the end of the eighteenth century, the old traditions of miniature painting in books and interior decoration in buildings were dying. In the course of the nineteenth century, they were replaced in the more Westernized Islamic countries by a new art and architecture that was first influenced and then dominated by European patterns. As early as the mid-eighteenth century, the great Nuruosmaniye Mosque in Istanbul shows strong Italian baroque influences in its ornamentation. The presence of European elements in something as central as an imperial cathedral mosque reveals a notable faltering of cultural self-confidence.

This became more evident in the course of the nineteenth and twentieth centuries. The old arts of miniature and calligraphy lingered on for a while, but those who practiced them, with few exceptions, lacked both originality and prestige. Their place in the artistic self-expression of society was taken by European-style painters, working in oils on canvas. Architecture, too, even mosque architecture, conformed in the main to European artistic notions, as well as to the inevitable European techniques. More recently, there has been an attempt to return to traditional Islamic patterns, but often this takes the form of a conscious neoclassicism. Only in one respect were Islamic norms generally retained, and that was in the slow and reluctant acceptance of sculpture, seen as a violation of the Islamic ban on graven images. One of the main grievances against such secularist modernizers as Kemal Atatürk in Turkey and the Shah in Iran was their practice of installing statues of themselves in public places. This was seen as no better than pagan idolatry.

The westernization of art was paralleled in literature, though at a somewhat later date. From the mid-nineteenth century onward, traditional literary forms were neglected, except among die-hard circles with limited intellectual impact. In their place came new forms and ideas from Europe—the novel and the short story, replacing the traditional tale and apologue; the essay and the newspaper article; and new forms and themes that have transformed modern poetry in Arabic, Persian, and Turkish alike. Even the language in which modern literature is written has been extensively and irreversibly changed, under the influence of European discourse.

The change is least noticeable in music, where the impact of European art music is still relatively small. In Turkey, where European influence has lasted longest and gone deepest, there are talented performers, some of them with international reputations, and composers working in the European manner. Istanbul and Ankara are now on the concert circuit, and there are audiences large enough and faithful enough to make it worthwhile. Elsewhere in the Islamic world, those who compose, perform, or even listen to European music are still relatively few. Music in the various traditional modes is still being composed and performed at a high level, and it is accepted and appreciated by the vast majority of the population. Of late, there has been some penetration of the more popular types of Western music, but even these are in the main limited to comparatively small groups in the larger cities. Music is perhaps the profoundest and most intimate expression of a culture, and it is natural that it should be the last to yield to alien influences.

Another highly visible sign of European influence is in clothing. That Muslim armies use modern equipment and weaponry may be ascribed to necessity, and there are ancient traditions declaring it lawful to imitate the infidel enemy in order to defeat him. But that the officers of these armies wear fitted tunics and peaked caps cannot be so justified and has a significance at once cultural and symbolic. When the pagan Mongol armies conquered the lands of Islam in the thirteenth century, even the Muslim armies that resisted them adopted Mongol dress and accoutrements, and let their hair flow long and loose in the Mongol style. These were the habiliments of victory, and it was natural that others should seek to adopt them. It was not until some time later, when the Mongols themselves had embraced Islam, that a sultan of Egypt ordered his officers to shear their locks, abandon their Mongol dress, and return to traditional Islamic attire. In the nineteenth century, the Ottomans, followed by other Muslim states, adopted European-style uniforms for both officers and men, and European harness for their horses. Only the headgear remained un-Westernized, and for good reason. Traditionally, in the Middle East, headgear had served as a kind of emblem or sign by which men indicated their religious, ethnic, or even professional identity. They wore it as a badge throughout their lives, and it was carved in stone over their graves. The hat, with peak, visor, or brim, was seen as characteristic of the European and served to indicate him both in miniature painting and in popular shows. Such hats were particularly unsuited for Muslims, since they would obstruct the rituals of Islamic prayer. After the Kemalist revolution in Turkey, even this last bastion of Islamic conservatism fell. The Turkish army, along with the general population, adopted European hats and caps, and before long, they were followed by the armies and eventually even many civilians in almost all other Muslim states. Belted tunics and peaked caps are still worn in the armies of Libya, Saudi Arabia, and the Islamic Republic of Iran, and there has as yet been no movement to return to traditional Islamic dress for men.

The position is different for women. During the nineteenth and early twentieth centuries, the Europeanization of female attire was slower, later, and more limited. It was strongly resisted and affected a much smaller portion of the population. At many levels of society, where the wearing of Western clothes by men became normal, women still kept to traditional dress. Even Kemal Atatürk, the most ruthless of Westernizers and a pioneer of women's rights in the Islamic world, dealt differently with the two cases. For men, the abandonment of traditional headgear and the adoption of European hats was promulgated and enforced by law. Women were urged and encouraged to abandon the veil but never compelled to do so. One of the most noticeable consequences of the Islamic revival has been a reversal of this trend and a return, by women though not by men, to traditional attire.

For men and for women alike, the interlude of freedom was too long, and its effects too profound, for it to be forgotten. Despite many reverses, European-style democracy is not yet dead in the Islamic lands, and there are some signs of a revival. In Turkey, after a military intervention that halted a slide to anarchy, there has been a determined effort to restore parliamentary and constitutional government, with free elections and a free press. In Egypt, after a period of sometimes harsh military dictatorship, there has been a gradual return to a freer society, with contested elections, an opposition press, and a relatively liberal economy. In a few other countries, there have been steps, still rather tentative, toward liberalization. As the era of Western European domination recedes from memory to history, and as Western European ideas and European ways come to be better understood and appreciated, one may hope that the long record of strife will at last come to an end.

In the year 1693, when the Sacra Liga was still waging its successful war against the retreating Ottomans, an English Quaker called William Penn, the founder of the city of Philadelphia and the colony of Pennsylvania, wrote a little book, *An Essay Towards the Present and Future Peace of Europe*, in which he proposed an organization of European states, to arbitrate disputes and thus prevent wars. Remarkably, for a man of his time, William Penn suggested that Turkey be included in this European association, the only condition for acceptance being that the Turks renounce Islam and adopt Christianity. In the twentieth century, such a religious requirement, though still impossible, was, it seemed, no longer necessary. All the independent Muslim states existing at the time joined the Europe-based League of Nations. More recently, several Muslim nations have sought and been accorded associate membership of the European Economic Community. Turkey, legally a lay state but overwhelmingly Muslim in population and sentiment, has even applied for full membership. Much will depend, for the future attitudes both of the Turks and the other Islamic peoples, on the treatment accorded to that application.

Recent years have seen a major change—only the second such in many centuries—in the relationship between European Christendom and Middle Eastern Islam. For more than a thousand years, from the first irruption of the Muslim Arabs into Christendom in the seventh century to the second Turkish Muslim siege of Vienna in 1683, the pattern of the relationship between the two was one of Muslim advance and Christian retreat, and the issue of the struggle was the possession of Europe. From time to time, there were Christian rallies and advances— some of them permanent, like the recovery of the Iberian Peninsula and Sicily; others temporary, like the partial and limited recovery of the lost lands of Christendom in the Levant. The age of the discoveries brought an expansion of European trade in Asia and Africa, but it was a long time before trade was translated into power, and even longer before this power was extended farther from Asia and Africa to the Islamic heartlands in the Middle East and North Africa. Almost until the end of the seventeenth century, Europe was still under attack, and the Islamic heartlands were still inviolate, a region in which Europeans could enter, travel, and trade only by the revocable consent of the sultans and of the shahs.

The decisive change began with the Turkish defeat at Vienna and the subsequent withdrawal, culminating in the Treaty of

Karlowitz of 1699—the first ever to be imposed by a victorious Europe on a vanquished Turkey. For the next two and a half centuries, the pattern was one of European advance and Islamic retreat, involving the defeat and ultimate disappearance of the sultans and the shahs, the penetration and domination of their dominions, and the division of much of the Islamic world into European dependencies and spheres of influence.

Today, a second such major change is in progress. European economic domination has ended and in some measure been reversed, and once again, as in classical Ottoman times, it is Middle Eastern wealth and the need for Middle Eastern markets that influence, perhaps even determine, European policies. There is a reversal, too, in the military balance. Until the end of the Second World War, the European powers were in military domination of the region and even fought their own European battles on Middle Eastern soil. This, too, is now reversed, and Middle Eastern interests, in a different form of warfare, wage their conflicts on improvised European battlefields, both against Europe and against each other.

Perhaps more important than any of these, in the long run, is the new, massive presence in Western Europe of practicing Muslims, coming from North Africa and the Middle East, from Turkey, and from as far away as the Indian subcontinent. For the time being, the vast majority of these are immigrants or guest workers, and their political impact, though growing, is limited. But their children will be native-born and will be, and feel themselves to be, Europeans. In Britain and France, they will be citizens as of right, and even in Germany, where the laws of nationality are somewhat different, it will not be possible, in the long run, to deny them the citizenship to which they will feel that they are entitled. The emergence of a population, many millions strong, of Muslims born and educated in Western Europe will have immense and unpredictable consequences for Europe, for Islam, and for the relations between them.

THREE

Religion and Politics in Islam and Judaism

ET ME BEGIN WITH A QUOTATION. MORE THAN TWO hundred years ago, in the year 1799, a man called Mirza Abü Ṭālib Khan went on a visit to London. His origins were in Iranian Azerbaijan. He was born and lived in India, and his purpose no doubt was to go to see the homeland of the people who were at that time becoming the rulers of India. His book is quite long, and it was, as far as I am aware, the first and for some time the only description by a Muslim visitor of the functioning of governmental institutions in a Western democracy.

Mirza Abü Ṭālib Khan's book is very lengthy and quite fascinating. Among the places he visited was the House of Commons, which he describes in obvious bewilderment, for the instruction of his readers. His opening remarks are not very complimentary; the debate between the opposing sides of the House, he says, reminds him somewhat of a sight commonly seen in India, of two trees with parrots sitting on their branches screeching at each other across the road.

Then he goes on to explain the purpose of this extraordinary institution. It has, he says, three principal functions: the collection of taxes, the supervision of contractors, and the general supervision of the affairs of government. And then a little later in the book, at another point, he mentions another function of this body, which had previously no doubt escaped his attention. He observes, with obvious astonishment, that one of the functions of this House of Commons was to make laws, and to explain this extraordinary phenomenon to his readers, he points out that the English, unlike the Muslims, had not accepted a divine law—a divine, eternal, immutable law—and were therefore reduced to the expedient of making their own laws, which, he says, they did in accordance with the necessities of the time and circumstances, the general state of affairs, and the experience of their judges. This is not at all bad for a complete newcomer, as a summing up of the way that laws were made.

In this description and his comments, Mirza Abü Ṭālib Khan had laid his finger on one of the essential differences between Islam and Christendom as political systems, as political ideas—a difference that affects almost all aspects of law. For the Muslim, the law was the divine law, the *sharī'a*, a word that means a path toward something and is therefore an almost exact literal equivalent of the Jewish term *halakha*. And one might add, of course, that one of the main sources of the Sharī'a was Iraq, home of the Babylonian Talmud. The Sharī'a came some generations later, but in the same region, and with a remarkable amount in common.

In principle, there was no legislative power in the Muslim state and therefore no need for legislative assemblies. Now, all over Christendom, there is some kind of assembly, more or less democratic, ranging from the English House of Commons to the Nazi Reichstag or the Supreme Soviet, but nevertheless some kind of assembly brought together by some kind of rules with the function of making and, when necessary, repealing or amending the law. In fact, of course, Muslim governments did make and change laws. They could not carry on through more than a millennium of history with just the same basic legal principles that they had at the beginning. But the legislative process was, so to speak, surreptitious or, rather, disguised; it comes in the form of commentary and interpretation by the jurists or in the form of regulation by governments, both ostensibly for the clarification and application of the divine and eternal law.

This is part of a larger difference, and here I would like to quote a passage from a real connoisseur of political institutions, Alexis de Tocqueville, who also knew something about Islam. He spent some time in Algeria; he wrote some reports for the French parliament on the situation in Algeria, as well as his very famous book about the United States. Writing in 1835, de Tocqueville says:

> Mohammad brought down from heaven and placed in the Qur'ān not only religious doctrines, but also political maxims, civil and criminal laws, and scientific theories. The Gospels, in contrast, speak only of the general relations between man and God and among men. Apart from this they offer no teaching and impose no belief. This alone, among a thousand other reasons, suffices to show that the first of these two religions [that is to say, Islam] could not long dominate in times of enlightenment and democracy while the second is destined to prevail.

He, of course, has his own ax to grind. But the point he makes about the incompatibility of eternal legislation with the functioning of democratic institutions is an important one that bears closer consideration.

So far, I have been talking about Islam and Christendom, but in the title of this lecture the word *Judaism* occurs, and where does that come in? Judaism, like Christianity and Islam, is a religion and a culture, but unlike them it is not a civilization. Christianity is a religion; Christendom is a civilization. In speaking of Islam, we use the same word for both, but the equivalent distinction is there. Judaism has been a component of both. Most of the Jews, almost the overwhelming majority of Jews, have lived for the last fourteen centuries either under Christian or under Muslim rule. They have been, shall we say, a subculture within Christian civilization or within Muslim civilization. There were small and isolated groups of Jews in Hindu India and in China, but they had little significance either in the history of the Jews or in the history of those countries. Significant Jewish history, creative Jewish achievement, was entirely in the lands of Christendom and of Islam, and it is these two different traditions that we see coming together in Israel at the present day.

It has now become customary in the Western world to speak of the Judeo-Christian tradition; the reality is old, but the expression is new. It dates from modern times; in earlier times, it would have been equally resented on both sides of the hyphen. We do not normally speak of the Judeo-Islamic tradition, but one could do so with equal justification. There are historically two kinds of Jews, the Jews of Islam and the Jews of Christendom. One hears a great deal in Israel at the present time of the encounter — I choose my word carefully — between Ashkenazic and Sephardic Jews. That isn't really the point. *Ashkenaz* and *Sepharad* conventionally in medieval Hebrew mean Germany and Spain, respectively. Jews from Iraq, Iran, and Afghanistan have no more to do with Spain than with Poland; indeed, they are rather nearer to Poland geographically. That's not the point. Minor differences of ritual between these two groups of Jews are irrelevant. We get a little closer to reality with those who see it and put it in fashionable modern parlance as the encounter between Euro-American and Afro-Asian Jews, but that's not really the point either. The encounter is, if you will forgive me for putting it this way, between the Christian Jews and the Muslim Jews, using these terms not in a religious but in a civilizational sense.

This affects Jewish life even in the most intimate details. Before coming into this room, I looked through the exhibition of *rimmonim* (Jewish ritural objects) at the other end of this building. There are *rimmonim* from all over the Jewish world. And it is rather striking that those that come from Muslim countries have a suggestion of a mosque and a minaret about them, and those that come from Europe are rather reminiscent of a Gothic cathedral. We see the same thing in even such an intimate matter as marriage, where the Jews of Islam were permitted to practice polygamy, though not concubinage, whereas the Jews of Christendom were limited to one wife—one wife at a time, that is.

More relevantly for our purpose, we see it also in—I hesitate, but I use the word—the clergy, or should we say the professional men of religion. And if we look at the professional men of religion and others from both camps, from the Christian Jews and the Muslim Jews, we see bishops and muftis, cardinals and ayatollahs, and looking on the seamier sides, inquisitors and assassins. The Jewish people have lived in both and have been profoundly affected—more than affected, molded—by both these two major civilizations.

Let me turn for a moment from the larger topic of the Jewish people to the narrower, more closely defined topic of the land of Israel. Israel is now celebrating its fiftieth year as a state. Fifty years in the life of an individual is very important; fifty years in the life of a society, of a polity, is a fleeting moment. Before that, it was British for thirty years and not even effectively controlled for the whole of that period. Before that, it was Ottoman for four hundred years, and before the four hundred years of Ottoman rule, almost a thousand years of other Muslim rulers.

All this, of course, has left its mark. To a surprising extent, the state of Israel is a successor state, not only of the British but also of the Ottoman Empire; in unequal proportions, no doubt, but Israel in its system of government, its social habits, and the rest preserves a great deal of the Ottoman system, partly of what we might call the classical Ottoman system and rather more of the reformed Ottoman system of the nineteenth and early twentieth centuries. Indeed, I would say that the Ottoman heritage is more conservatively maintained in Israel than in any of the other Ottoman successor states that I can think of, certainly more than in the Balkan states, very much more than in the Turkish republic, and even, in some respects, more than in the Arab successor states of the Ottoman Empire.

The Ottoman Empire maintained and in the nineteenth century systematized what is called the *millet* system, whereby each religious community lived under its own chiefs, under its own laws, conducting its own education. In the case of the Jews—and the same thing happened for others—the rabbinate even enjoyed the legal power to enforce their rules. In the Ottoman Empire, Jews could be punished with imprisonment, fines, or flogging for offenses against the rabbinic law, for example, desecrating the Sabbath, the dietary laws, and the like. This system carries with it a very important element, sometimes known as the law of personal status, that is to say, principally marriage, divorce, and inheritance. In the Ottoman Empire, these were entirely the preserve of the religious communities. You could have in the same street, living side by side, Muslims, Christians, and Jews. Muslims were allowed to practice polygamy and concubinage; Jews were allowed to practice polygamy but not concubinage; Christians were forbidden to practice either, and Christians under Ottoman rule could be severely punished, by the authority of the priest, for doing things that were perfectly legal for the majority and dominant community in the empire.

One sees the survival of Ottoman practice in this modern state of Israel, even in attire. I have again and again been struck by the practice of some Israeli rabbis of wearing the costume of a middle-ranking Ottoman functionary of the late nineteenth century.

In talking of Christendom and the politics of Christendom, it is customary to speak of the problems of church and state, the relations between church and state. The word *church* in English and in all the other languages of Christendom has two different meanings. It is a building, a place of worship; it is also an institution, the church, which means something quite different. Anyone who knows anything about Christian practice and Christian history will know what is meant when one speaks of the church as an institution. One does not speak of the mosque or the synagogue in the same way, and if one does, it is through ignorance and false analogy. There is a story that is told of an Anglican clergyman who was what's called a Judaist, that's to say a scholarly specialist in the field of Judaic studies, and he wrote a book called *The Systematic Theology of the Synagogue*. It was reviewed by a rabbi who began his review with these words (I quote from memory, but I think correctly): "First, there is no such thing as 'the synagogue' and if there were, it wouldn't have a theology and if it did, it wouldn't be systematic." You will sometimes find people speaking of "the synagogue" or "the mosque" in a sense analogous to the Christian use of "the church," but this is usually due to ignorance or most recently, to a kind of cultural assimilation; it doesn't really convey any precise meaning.

The basic Christian text is Matthew 22:21: "Render therefore unto Caesar the things which are Caesar's; and unto God the things that are God's." This verse has been variously interpreted, but it has generally been understood to recognize two distinct areas in society, one concerned with politics, with power, and the other concerned with religion, with worship, each with its own institution, personnel, and rules. If we look through Christian history, there have always been these two—sometimes joined, sometimes separate; sometimes in cooperation, sometimes in conflict; sometimes one prevailing, sometimes the other; but always two distinct authorities representing the *imperium* and the *sacerdotium*, the imperial Power and the priestly power. In Islam and in Judaism, there is no equivalent distinction.

Let me go into this in greater detail. To discuss religion and politics and the interplay of the two in these societies, we have two different sources of information. One is the literary record, the immense body of writings, practical and theoretical, discussing the state, the nature of the state, the church, the nature of the church, and so on. In addition to the theoretical literature, both Christendom and Islam offer a wide range of practical experience—we have the long historical record of how church and state, the religious and the political power, reacted in these two societies. There are, after all, three Christendoms, Orthodox, Catholic, and Protestant. There are two Islams, Sunni and Shīʿa. I omit the smaller groups in both religions.

We can look at this question through a long period of such history, fourteen centuries of Islamic history, sixteen centuries of Christian history—and you may ask why just sixteen centuries, why not two thousand years? Because it wasn't until the year 313 that Emperor Constantine formally declared himself a Christian and established Christianity as the religion of the state. It wasn't until then that the Christian religion became involved with the exercise of power.

The Muslim record was quite different. Muhammad was, so to speak, his own Constantine. He established a state during his lifetime, in which he did the things that statesmen do. He commanded armies, he made war, he made peace, he collected taxes, and he dispensed justice, and so whereas the Christian memory is of centuries of persecution and martyrdom, ending finally in the capture of the state, the Islamic sacred scriptures and memories have a total identification of faith and power during the lifetime of the founder.

What about the Jews? The Jews are obviously a much smaller group but still have a very extensive literature dealing with the subject—political literature, both practical and theoretical. But most of it is theoretical rather than practical for the very good reason that they had no practice on which to base it. It tends to be abstract and perhaps even messianic at times. The one practical principle that matters is the one summed up in the rabbinic formula *dina demalkhuta dina*; in other words, what the government says, goes—a free translation, but I think it's not inaccurate. The Jewish experience of sovereignty was limited. The memory of the ancient Jewish states was too remote; the history of the modern Jewish state too brief. One state, fifty years, as a sample is not really enough to make judgments comparable with those we can make on Christendom and Islam. It is too little to permit even the most tentative generalization.

This, however, will not deter me. There was some experience and there were individual Jews who played a part in the political process, but they are very few and when they got to that point, they were, generally speaking, de-Judaized; it was not as Jews or in any Jewish sense that they played a part in the political process. There was some Jewish political life in those countries where a measure of communal autonomy was permitted. I quoted the example of the Ottoman *millet*; one finds similar things in Eastern Europe at times. But this kind of communal authority was always limited, delegated, revocable, and, most relevant of all, imitative. In the words of Heinrich Heine: "Wie es Christelt sich, so jüdelt es sich." The same might be said of Jewish communal institutions in Muslim countries.

The sacred history of the three religions exemplifies these differences: Moses was forbidden to enter the Promised Land; Jesus was crucified; Muḥammad conquered his holy land, and it was his enemies and not he who were put to death. The major biblical themes are, in the earlier books, slavery and liberation; in the later books, exile and return. And in postbiblical times, the dominating idea is of the fence to the Torah, whereby the rabbinical successors of the Old Testament tried to preserve something by elaborate regulations. They seem to have seen themselves as the custodians and guarantors of Jewish identity and continuity without a state or even in spite of the state, as was often necessary. There was no equivalent of the church.

The Muslim experience is somewhat different. There was no need for a church since the establishment, so to speak, of a community and polity in the lifetime of the founder, who ruled as both prophet and sovereign. His successors were not prophets, but they did inherit his religious authority. The Muslim theory of the caliphate sees the head of the state not indeed as a spiritual chief, but as a religious chief. Sometimes he has been described as pope and emperor in one, but that is misleading. He did not claim the powers of the papacy but certainly reigned as head imam of a religiously defined community, and there was no need for a church in the Christian sense as a separate institution.

In classical Islam, there was no priesthood, no sacraments, no hierarchy. The men of religion, the ulema, rather like the rabbis on whom they are in some sense modeled, were seen as scholars in religion and law, but in time they were, so to speak, professionalized. A system was introduced of training, with training certification—some kind of examination or testing, the result of which was the conferment of some kind of diploma or equivalent. With training and certification comes pay, since even ulema have to make a living. And with pay come grades, and with grades comes a measure of hierarchy.

At first, in the early centuries of Islam, the dominant attitude expressed among the ulema was mistrust of the state. The state was seen as a necessary evil but an evil nevertheless. There is a dictum often repeated by the early writers, *"Al-Jannatu wa'l-sulṭān lā yajtami'ān,"* or "heaven and government don't go together." If you have to function in the government—somebody has to do it—it's too bad, but your chances of going to heaven are minimal.

But then during the later Middle Ages, there was a change. Islam and the Islamic world faced a threefold threat: the attack of the Crusaders from the west, the attack of the heathen Mongols from the east, and the attack of Shīʿa and Ismāʿīlīs and other forms of heresy from within. In confronting this triple attack, the state and the religious hierarchy came closer together, and we have a new situation in which the religious hierarchy was in a sense taken over by the state and became part of the apparatus of the state, but nevertheless a separate and independent organization with its own rules, capable of defying the state. It is true that in the Ottoman Empire, the chief mufti of the capital, with the title of sheikh al-Islam, had the theoretical right to depose the sultan. According to Muslim legal doctrine, sovereignty is contractual, and the head of the state holds his office by a contract between him and the community, a contract that imposes duties on both parties, the ruler and the ruled. And if the ruler for any reason fails to carry out his part of the contract or, worse still, if he acts in an evil way, then the contract lapses, and obedience to the ruler is no longer obligatory. But of course, anyone familiar with any Western constitutional system will immediately ask who is to decide, what is the testing device for this constitutional constraint? There is a saying of the Prophet often repeated: "There is no obedience in sin"; in other words, if the ruler orders something sinful, the duty of obedience, which otherwise prevails, lapses.

But who is to decide? Never at any time did they devise a constitutional testing device because there were no parliaments, no assemblies of any kind, no legislative function, and no legislative bodies. The Ottoman sultan could be deposed by an order of the chief mufti. The usual procedure was to draw up a question, present it to the chief mufti, and say, "If a sultan does this, this, this, and this, which is contrary to the Holy Law, may he be deposed?" And the chief mufti would say yes, he may be deposed. In practice, this simply meant a successful coup d'état. An impatient prince, a mutinous general, a rebellious governor, or whoever it might be would take over and, in order to legalize the coup d'état, would obtain the necessary fatwa from the chief mufti. This may look like a constitutional testing device, and to some extent it did have a constraining effect, but not really.

Let us turn for a moment and have another look at the Christian situation. The ongoing struggle between these two powers that coexisted in Christendom was expressed in the medieval struggle between the pope and the emperor, representing the supreme ecclesiastical authority and the supreme political and military authority, and, in a sense, was preceded by the earlier struggle between Constantinople and Rome. It was followed by the Reformation and the emergence of a new form of Christianity, Protestantism, with a very different approach to the whole question of the relationship between religion and politics.

This gave rise to the great wars of religion in Christendom, which have no equivalent in the history of Islam. There is a split in Islam between the Sunnis and the Shīʻa, but it is totally different from the split between Protestants and Catholics or even from the schism between Catholics and Orthodox. Although sometimes there were struggles, even wars, between the Ottoman sultan and the Persian shah, one of whom was Sunni and the other Shīʻa, this wasn't the issue. There is no true equivalent to the wars of religion and the persecutions that were part of them among Muslims, nor has there so far been a Protestant-style reformation in Islam—though the creation in Iran of an authoritarian religious institution, complete with hierarchy, episcopate, and inquisition, may provoke one.

The final solution that was found to these wars of religion in Christendom was a new doctrine—separation of church and state. This served a double purpose: on the one hand, to prevent the political power from interfering in matters of religion, and on the other hand, to prevent the religious hierarchy from using the political power of the state to enforce its purposes.

This practice and the later doctrine of separation of church and state in Christendom was a council of despair. Winston Churchill once said that you may trust the people to do the sensible thing after they exhausted all the other possibilities. Separation, I think, was accepted after a long, bitter, and bloody struggle in the wars of religion.

Islam had none of this. There were no struggles of pope and emperor. There was no pope; the caliph, and later the sultan, was emperor with considerable religious authority. There was no Reformation, though from time to time, there have been signs of an incipient reformation that so far have not led anywhere. And the notion of a separation was totally alien until very recently.

The new phase begins with the impact in the Islamic world of the ideas of the French Revolution. The French Revolution was the first movement of ideas in Europe that did not have a Christian label on it. All previous movements of ideas were, to a greater or lesser extent, Christian and therefore discounted in advance, and so, for example, such major European developments as the Renaissance, the Reformation, and the scientific revolution had no impact at all in the Islamic world. The French Revolution was not Christian; it even, to some extent, presented itself as anti-Christian and was therefore assured of a respectful hearing.

It also intruded itself more directly with the French invasion of Egypt in 1798. After that, there was an opening to the West and a much closer acquaintance with Western institutions. Mirza Abū Ṭālib Khan was the first, but there were many more in the course of the nineteenth century, and we find them interested in particular in three models: the French model of the revolutionary republic, the English model of limited constitutional authority under the Crown, and the German-Austrian model of the Rechtsstaat, the state according to law, without worrying too much about such nonsense as free institutions.

The Ottoman reforms of the nineteenth century, and similar movements on a smaller scale in other countries, brought a

number of changes. One of the most important was the bureau-
cratization of the ulema, who became, even more than ever
before, part of the apparatus of the state, indeed salaried officials
of the state. More important than that was the gradual secularization of the laws, the introduction of a civil code, a commercial
code, and later a criminal code that supplement and eventually
supplant the holy law.

We still see different variants of this in the Islamic world of
the present time. On the one hand, there are countries that are,
or claim to be, totally traditional. In Saudi Arabia, for example,
there is no constitution; they say the Qur'ān is our constitution;
there are no law codes, because the Sharī'a is the law. One finds
this also in some other countries where Sharī'a law has been
retained or reintroduced.

There are compromises, in countries like Egypt, where some
secular laws have been introduced, but other areas, notably the
laws of personal status, have remained subject to Sharī'a. And
then there are the totally modern states like Turkey and the
former Soviet republics where Islam is, so to speak, entirely
disestablished, where Sharī'a law has no legal force or validity
whatsoever in any area.

This has become the major cause, the major argument, of the
groups that we have got into the habit of calling fundamentalists. The name is an unfortunate one, a misleading one. The
term *fundamentalist* is not just Christian; one can be more precise
about it—it is American Protestant. It dates from the early years
of the twentieth century when it was used to designate certain
American Protestant churches and to differentiate them from
the mainstream Protestant churches. The two points on which
American Protestant fundamentalists—that is, those who took
out the patent on the name—differed from other Christians was,
first, their rejection of liberal theology, which had become quite
popular in most of the other churches, and, second, their insis-
tence on the literal divinity and inerrancy of the Bible (in the
King James English version, of course).

These were important issues for Protestants. They were not issues at all in the Muslim world. Liberal theology has been an issue in the past, it may again become an issue in the future, but it is not an issue at the present time. And as for the divinity and inerrancy of scripture, this is a basic Muslim dogma about which there is no argument at all among believing Muslims.

The issue is something quite different, and it is basically the issue of Sharīʿa. The so-called Islamic fundamentalists have, as the main thrust of their attack, what they see as the secularization or, as they put it, the paganization of the state. This came out very clearly in the interrogation of the group of people who murdered the late president of Egypt, Anwar Sadat. There is a widespread assumption that Sadat was murdered because he made peace with Israel; this is not correct. We have detailed, published reports of the interrogation of his murderers, and they make it quite clear that while they didn't like the peace with Israel or the opening to the United States, this wasn't their issue. This was, so to speak, an epiphenomenon; the real accusation against Sadat was that under the guise of Islam and with a pretense of being a Muslim, he was de-Islamizing the Egyptian state by removing the Sharīʿa and replacing it with foreign-inspired secular laws in important areas of public life. When the leader of the group of murderers, in the moments between the crime and his arrest, exclaimed, "I have killed Pharaoh," he was not accusing Sadat of being soft on Israel; he was accusing him of being a pagan tyrant.

The complaint of Khomeini against the shah was more or less the same. This has been the issue of the fundamentalists in all the Muslim countries: the maintenance or restoration of the Sharīʿa. There are countries where the Sharīʿa had been removed or considerably reduced, and where it has been reintroduced and its scope greatly extended, for example, Afghanistan, Pakistan, Sudan, and most recently, Iran. So we have two models in the Islamic world, the Turkish model and the Iranian model: in Turkey, complete modernization, secularization, the disestablishment and control of religion, and the exclusion of religion from any kind of role in public and political life, and at the opposite extreme, the Islamic Republic of Iran, which has made as its main program the reintroduction of Sharī'a law in all its aspects and the strict enforcement of all its provisions. We might call these two programs Kemalism and Khomeinism, secular democracy and Islamic theocracy. We know that in Turkey a considerable minority would like to re-Islamize the state; in the last election, they got slightly more than 20 percent of the vote. We do not know what proportion of Iranians would prefer a secular democracy because in an Islamic theocracy, it is not permitted to express that preference. But one gets the impression that it is not unimportant.

Let me turn again to the Jews. And here it seems to me that the Jews in Israel, and to a lesser extent elsewhere, face the same choice between a religiously dominated state and a secular state as do the Turks and the Persians and the rest of the peoples of Islam, and that in making the necessary adjustments in this country, too, there is a choice between Kemalism and Khomeinism— and one sees both Kemalists and Khomeinists engaged in public life in this country. In the past, separation of church and state was seen as a Christian solution for a Christian problem, irrelevant to both Muslims and Jews—especially to Jews; separation between church and state meant nothing to people who had neither a state nor a church. Today they have a state, and they are rapidly acquiring a church. Relations between the two are becoming an issue.

In every observant Jewish household, every Saturday evening there is a little ceremony called *havdala*, or separation. Separation of what? Well, the text tells us, "*bayn qodesh le-ḥol*," separation between, shall we say, sacred and profane. It seems to me that this, though intended for another matter, could provide an authentically Jewish textual basis for the next step that needs to be taken.

FOUR

Islam and Liberal Democracy

     THERE HAS BEEN MUCH DISCUSSION OF LATE, BOTH inside and outside the Islamic world, about those elements in the Islamic past and those factors in the Muslim present that are favorable and unfavorable to the development of liberal democracy. From a historical perspective it would seem that of all the non-Western civilizations in the world, Islam offers the best prospects for Western-style democracy. Historically, culturally, religiously, it is the closest to the West, sharing much—though by no means all—of the Judeo-Christian and Greco-Roman heritage that helped to form our modern civilization. From a political perspective, however, Islam seems to offer the worst prospects for liberal democracy. Of the forty-six sovereign states that make up the international Islamic Conference, only one, the Turkish Republic, can be described as a democracy in Western terms, and even there the path to freedom has been beset by obstacles. Of the remainder, some have never tried democracy; others have tried it and failed; a few have experimented with the idea of sharing, though not of relinquishing, power.

    Can liberal democracy work in a society inspired by Islamic beliefs and principles and shaped by Islamic experience and tradition? It is of course for Muslims, primarily and perhaps exclusively, to interpret and reinterpret the pristine original message of their faith, and to decide how much to retain, and in what form, of the rich accumulated heritage of fourteen centuries of Islamic history and culture. Not all Muslims give the same answers to the question posed above, but much will depend on the answer that prevails.

THE PROD OF WEAKNESS

On 14 December 1909, the Ottoman sultan Mehmed V, in a speech from the throne delivered to the Ottoman parliament, spoke of the commitment of his administration to "constitutional and consultative government...the way of security and salvation prescribed by the noble *sharī'a* and by both reason and tradition." The content of the speech and the manner of its delivery reflected the new situation after the Young Turk Revolution of 1908 and the suppression of the counterrevolutionary mutiny in the spring of 1909. Under the restored constitution the Ottoman Empire had become a constitutional monarchy, and the speech that the Sultan presented, British-style, to his parliament was written for him by his ministers, whose policies it expressed. The language used is interesting and revealing. "Constitution" is *meşrutiyet*, a term coined in the nineteenth century to denote a new procedure; "consultation" is *meşveret*, an old term with many associations derived from both Ottoman political usage and Islamic political literature. The Islamic association implied by the use of this term is made explicit by the citation of "the noble *sharī'a*" and of "reason and tradition," *'akl ve-nakl*, a formula commonly used by Muslim theologians. The desire to borrow or imitate Western institutions perceived as useful, and to present them as somehow representing a return to authentic and original Islamic principles, is characteristic of most nineteenth-century and some twentieth-century Islamic reformers. The desire for such change arose in the main from a growing awareness of Western strength and wealth contrasted with Muslim weakness and poverty. The discovery or invention of Islamic antecedents was seen as necessary to make such political changes acceptable to the people of a proud and deeply conservative society with old and strong religio-political traditions of its own—these last including a profound contempt for the unbeliever and all his ways. It is not easy to accept instruction in matters as fundamental as the conduct of state from those one has long been accustomed to regard as benighted and unenlightened.

Muslim awareness of weakness and defeat first achieved significant expression in the early eighteenth century, following the disastrous failure of the second siege of Vienna (1683) and the Treaty of Karlowitz (1699), the first imposed by a victorious enemy on a defeated Ottoman government. There had been earlier defeats and setbacks—the final expulsion of the Moors from Spain, the ending of the Tatar yoke in Russia, the establishment of the Western European maritime powers in the Muslim lands of South and Southeast Asia. But all these were in a sense peripheral and seem to have had little impact on the heartlands of Islam and the Middle East, where the Ottoman Empire, the last and in many ways the greatest of the Muslim military empires, continued to perform its task as the sword and shield of Islam in the long struggle against Christendom. For a while the awareness of weakness was in the main limited to the Ottoman governing elite, the first to bear the brunt of the changed balance of forces, while the rest of the population was still protected from both invasion and reality by the armed might of the Ottoman state, even in its decline a formidable military power. The terms of the discussion were similarly limited to military matters, to weapons and training and military organization, since for some time it was in these alone that Muslims experienced the growing superiority of the West. The events of the late eighteenth and early nineteenth centuries—the Russians in the Black Sea, the French in Egypt—made European superiority painfully obvious. This succession of military defeats was the more galling to the people of a religious society with a long history of political and military triumph, starting in the lifetime of its founder, and with a proud awareness of that sacred history.

In time there arose some among the reformers who argued that European military superiority derived from nonmilitary causes, and two in particular—one economic, the other political. Some identified the sources of Western power more specifically as industrialization and constitutional government. The Arab failures in the struggle against Israel, particularly in 1948 and in 1967, revived the great debate on what is wrong with Arab and, more broadly, Islamic society, and what can be done to put it right. Like the Turks after their failure to capture Vienna, so the Arabs after their failure to capture Jerusalem began by seeing this as a primarily military problem for which there was a military solution: bigger and better armies with bigger and better weapons. And when these bigger and better armies also failed, there was a growing willingness to listen to those who sought deeper causes and offered more radical solutions.

FUNDAMENTALISTS AND DEMOCRATS

There are many who see no need for any such change and would prefer to retain the existing systems, whether radical dictatorships or traditional autocracies, with perhaps some improvement in the latter. This preference for things as they are is obviously shared by those who rule under the present system and those who otherwise benefit, including foreign powers who are willing to accept and even support existing regimes as long as their own interests are safeguarded. But there are others who feel that the present systems are both evil and doomed and that new institutions must be devised and installed.

Proponents of radical change fall into two main groups—the so-called Islamic fundamentalists and the democrats. Each group includes a wide range of sometimes contending ideologies.

The term *fundamentalism* was used first in America and then in other predominantly Protestant countries to designate certain groups that diverge from the mainstream churches. The use of the term to designate Muslim movements is at best a loose analogy and can be very misleading. Reformist theology has at times in the past been an issue among Muslims; it is not now, and it is very far from the primary concerns of those who are called Muslim fundamentalists.

Those concerns are less with scripture and theology than with society, law, and government. As the Muslim fundamentalists see it, the community of Islam has been led into error by foreign infidels and Muslim apostates; the latter being the more dangerous and destructive. Under their guidance or constraint Muslims abandoned the laws and principles of their faith and instead adopted secular—that is to say, pagan—laws and values. All the foreign ideologies—liberalism, socialism, even nationalism—that set Muslim against Muslim are evil, and the Muslim world is now suffering the inevitable consequences of forsaking the God-given law and way of life that were vouchsafed to it. The answer is the old Muslim obligation of jihad: to wage holy war first at home, against the pseudo-Muslim apostates who rule, and then, having ousted them and re-Islamized society, to resume the greater role of Islam in the world. The return to roots, to authenticity, will always be attractive. It will be doubly appealing to those who daily suffer the consequences of the failed foreign innovations that were foisted on them.

For Islamic fundamentalists, democracy is obviously an irrelevance, and unlike the communist totalitarians, they rarely use or even misuse the word. They are, however, willing to demand and exploit the opportunities that a self-proclaimed democratic system by its own logic is bound to offer them. At the same time, they make no secret of their contempt for democratic political procedures and their intention to govern by Islamic rules if they gain power. Their attitude toward democratic elections has been summed up as "one man, one vote, once." This is not entirely accurate, at least not for the Iranians. The Islamic Republic of Iran has held contested elections and has suffered more freedom of debate and criticism in the press and in its parliament than is usual in most Muslim countries, but there are exacting and strictly enforced limitations on who may be a candidate, what groups may be formed, and what ideas may be expressed. It goes without saying that no questioning of the basic principles of the Islamic revolution or the republic is permitted.

Those who plead or fight for democratic reform in the Arab and other Islamic lands claim to represent a more effective, more authentic democracy than that of their failed predecessors, not restricted or distorted by some intrusive adjective, not nullified by a priori religious or ideological imperatives, not misappropriated by regional or sectarian or other sectional interests. In part their movement is an extension to the Middle East of the wave of democratic change that has already transformed the governments of many countries in southern Europe and Latin America; in part it is a response to the collapse of the Soviet Union and the new affirmation of democratic superiority through victory in the Cold War. To no small extent it is also a consequence of the growing impact of the U.S. democracy and of American popular culture in the Islamic lands.

For some time America was seen merely as an extension of Western Europe—part of the same civilization, speaking the same language as the greatest of the empires, professing the same religion, damned by the same fatal flaws. Closer acquaintance revealed profound differences between American and Western European democracy, giving the former an attraction that the latter never possessed.

There is, of course, the obvious difference that the United States has never exercised imperial authority over Arab lands. A consequence of this is the less obvious but in the long run vastly more important difference that Americans in general—albeit with some well-known exceptions—have not developed the imperial attitude that colored, and to some extent still colors, human relations between Britons and Frenchmen on the one hand and the peoples of their former possessions on the other. This has made possible for Americans the kind of informal, equal, person-to-person relationships with Middle Easterners that were, and to some extent still are, rarely possible for Europeans.

American popular culture and mores have penetrated far more deeply and widely in Middle Eastern society than was ever possible for the elitist cultures of Britain and France. This kind of relationship is further encouraged by westward migration. There are now millions of Britons of South Asian, and Frenchmen of North African, origin. But it will probably be a long time before they achieve the level of integration and acceptance already achieved by new Americans from the Middle East. These have already become an important part of the American political process; they may yet find a role in the political processes of their countries of origin.

It is precisely the catholicity, the assimilative power and attraction, of American culture that make it an object of fear and hatred among the self-proclaimed custodians of pristine, authentic Islam. For such as they, it is a far more deadly threat than any of its predecessors to the old values that they hold dear and to the power and influence those values give them. In the last chapter of the Quran, which ranks with the first among the best known and most frequently cited, the believer is urged to seek refuge with God "from the mischief of the insidious Whisperer who whispers in people's hearts...." Satan in the Quran is the adversary, the deceiver, above all the inciter and tempter who seeks to entice mankind away from the true faith. It is surely in this sense that the Ayatollah Khomeini called America the great Satan: Satan as enemy, but—more especially and certainly more plausibly for his people—also as source of enticement and temptation.

In these times of discontent and disappointment, of anger and frustration, the older appeals of nationalism and socialism and national socialism—the gifts of nineteenth- and twentieth-century Europe—have lost much of their power. Today only the democrats and the Islamic fundamentalists appeal to something more than personal or sectional loyalties. Both have achieved some limited success, partly by infiltrating the existing regimes, more often by frightening them into making some preemptive concessions. Successes have in the main been limited to the more traditional authoritarian regimes, which have made some symbolic gestures toward the democrats or the fundamentalists or both. Even the radical dictatorships, while admitting no compromise with liberal democracy, have in times of stress tried to appease and even to use Islamic sentiment.

There is an agonizing question at the heart of the present debate about democracy in the Islamic world: Is liberal democracy basically compatible with Islam, or is some measure of respect for law, some tolerance of criticism, the most that can be expected from autocratic governments? The democratic world contains many different forms of government—republics and monarchies, presidential and parliamentary regimes, secular states and established churches, and a wide range of electoral systems—but all of them share certain basic assumptions and practices that mark the distinction between democratic and undemocratic governments. Is it possible for the Islamic peoples to evolve a form of government that will be compatible with their own historical, cultural, and religious traditions and yet will bring individual freedom and human rights to the governed as these terms are understood in the free societies of the West?

No one, least of all the Islamic fundamentalists themselves, will dispute that their creed and political program are not compatible with liberal democracy. But Islamic fundamentalism is just one stream among many. In the fourteen centuries that have passed since the mission of the Prophet, there have been several such movements—fanatical, intolerant, aggressive, and violent. Led by charismatic religious figures from outside the establishment, they have usually begun by denouncing the perversion of the faith and the corruption of society by the false and evil Muslim rulers and leaders of their time. Sometimes these movements have been halted and suppressed by the ruling establishment. At other times they have gained power and used it to wage holy war, first at home, against those whom they saw as backsliders and apostates, and then abroad against the other enemies of the true faith. In time these regimes have been either ousted or, if they have survived, transformed—usually in a fairly short period—into something not noticeably better, and in some ways rather worse, than the old establishments that they had overthrown. Something of this kind has already happened in the Islamic Republic of Iran.

The question, therefore, is not whether liberal democracy is compatible with Islamic fundamentalism—clearly it is not—but whether it is compatible with Islam itself. Liberal democracy, however far it may have traveled, however much it may have been transformed, is in its origins a product of the West—shaped by a thousand years of European history, and beyond that by Europe's double heritage: Judeo-Christian religion and ethics; Greco-Roman statecraft and law. No such system has originated in any other cultural tradition; it remains to be seen whether such a system, transplanted and adapted in another culture, can long survive.

Leaving aside the polemical and apologetic arguments—that Islam, not Western liberalism, is the true democracy, or that Western liberalism itself derives from Islamic roots—the debate about Islam and liberal democracy has focused on a few major points.

GOD'S POLITY

Every civilization formulates its own idea of good government, and creates institutions through which it endeavors to put that idea into effect. Since classical antiquity these institutions in the West have usually included some form of council or assembly, through which qualified members of the polity participate in the formation, conduct, and, on occasion, replacement of the government. The polity may be variously defined; so, too, may be the qualifications that entitle a member of the polity to participate in its governance. Sometimes, as in the ancient Greek city, the participation of citizens may be direct. More often qualified participants will, by some agreed-upon and recurring procedure, choose some from among their own numbers to represent them. These assemblies are of many different kinds, with differently defined electorates and functions, often with some role in the making of decisions, the enactment of laws, and the levying of taxes.

The effective functioning of such bodies was made possible by the principle embodied in Roman law, and in systems derived from it, of the legal person—that is to say, a corporate entity that for legal purposes is treated as an individual, able to own, buy, or sell property, enter into contracts and obligations, and appear as either plaintiff or defendant in both civil and criminal proceedings. There are signs that such bodies existed in pre-Islamic Arabia. They disappeared with the advent of Islam, and from the time of the Prophet until the first introduction of Western institutions in the Islamic world there was no equivalent among the Muslim peoples of the Athenian boule, the Roman Senate, the Jewish Sanhedrin, the Icelandic Althing or the Anglo-Saxon Witenagemot, or of any of the innumerable parliaments, councils, synods, diets, chambers, and assemblies of every kind that flourished all over Christendom.

One obstacle to the emergence of such bodies was the absence of any legal recognition of corporate persons. There were some limited moves in the direction of recognition. Islamic commercial law recognizes various forms of partnership for limited business purposes. A *waqf*, a pious foundation, once settled is independent of its settlor and can in theory continue indefinitely, with the right to own, acquire, and alienate property. But these never developed beyond their original purposes, and at no point reached anything resembling the governmental, ecclesiastical, and private corporate entities of the West.

Thus almost all aspects of Muslim government have an intensely personal character. In principle, at least, there is no state, but only a ruler; no court, but only a judge. There is not even a *city* with defined powers, limits, and functions, but only an assemblage of neighborhoods, mostly defined by family, tribal, ethnic, or religious criteria, and governed by officials, usually military, appointed by the sovereign. Even the famous Ottoman imperial divan—the *divan-i humayun*—described by many Western visitors as a council, could more accurately be described as a meeting, on fixed days during the week, of high political, administrative, judicial, financial, and military officers, presided over in earlier times by the sultan, in later times by the grand vizier. Matters brought before the meeting were referred to the relevant member of the divan, who might make a recommendation. The final responsibility and decision lay with the sultan or the grand vizier.

One of the major functions of such bodies in the West, increasingly through the centuries, was legislation. According to Muslim doctrine, there was no legislative function in the Islamic state, and therefore no need for legislative institutions. The

Islamic state was in principle a theocracy—not in the Western sense of a state ruled by the church and the clergy, since neither existed in the Islamic world, but in the more literal sense of a polity ruled by God. For believing Muslims, legitimate authority comes from God alone, and the ruler derives his power not from the people, nor yet from his ancestors, but from God and the holy law. In practice, and in defiance of these beliefs, dynastic succession became the norm, but it was never given the sanction of the holy law. Rulers made rules, but these were considered, theoretically, as elaborations or interpretations of the only valid law—that of God, promulgated by revelation. In principle the state was God's state, ruling over God's people; the law was God's law; the army was God's army; and the enemy, of course, was God's enemy.

Without legislative or any other kind of corporate bodies, there was no need for any principle of representation or any procedure for choosing representatives. There was no occasion for collective decision, and no need therefore for any procedure for achieving and expressing it, other than consensus. Such central issues of Western political development as the conduct of elections and the definition and extension of the franchise therefore had no place in Islamic political evolution.

Not surprisingly, in view of these differences, the history of the Islamic states is one of almost unrelieved autocracy. The Muslim subject owed obedience to a legitimate Muslim ruler as a religious duty. That is to say, disobedience was a sin as well as a crime.

Modernization in the nineteenth century, and still more in the twentieth, far from reducing this autocracy, substantially increased it. On the one hand, modern technology, communications, and weaponry greatly reinforced the rulers' powers of surveillance, indoctrination, and repression. On the other hand, social and economic modernization enfeebled or abrogated the religious constraints and intermediate powers that had in various ways limited earlier autocracies. No Arab caliph or Turkish sultan of the past could ever have achieved the arbitrary and pervasive power wielded by even the pettiest of present-day dictators.

MONEY AND POWER

The impediments to the development of liberal institutions were not merely political. The small-scale autocracy of the home, especially the upper-class home, founded on polygamy, concubinage, and slavery, was preparation for an adult life of domination and acquiescence, and a barrier to the entry of liberal ideas. Women—particularly the mothers, sisters, wives, and daughters of rulers—have played a much more important role in Muslim history than is usually conceded by historians. But they were until very recently precluded from contributing to the development of their society in the way that a succession of remarkable women have contributed to the flowering of the West.

The economic basis of Western-style liberal democracy was early recognized in the West. British, American, and French democrats alike insisted on the right to property as one of the basic human rights that safeguard and are safeguarded by free institutions. It also forms an essential component of civil society as conceived by European thinkers. For some time the rise of socialist ideas, parties, and governments weakened the belief in private property as a liberal value. Recent events have done much to restore that belief.

Islamic law unequivocally recognizes the sanctity of private property, but Islamic history reveals a somewhat different picture, in which even a rich man's enjoyment of his property has never been safe from seizure or sequestration by the state. This chronic insecurity is symbolized in the architecture of the traditional Muslim city, in which neighborhoods, and even the houses of the wealthy, are turned inward, surrounded by high blank walls. Marx and Engels themselves recognized that their canonical sequence of ruling classes defined by production relationships might not apply to non-Western societies. They sketched the theory of what they called "the Asiatic mode of production," in which there was no effective private ownership of land, and consequently no class war—just a simple opposition between the terrorized mass of the population and the all-encompassing state power, bureaucratic and military.

Like many of their other insights, this is a caricature, not a portrait, but also like their other insights, it is not without some basis in reality. Comparing the relationship between property and power in the modern American and classical Middle Eastern systems, one might put the difference this way: in America one uses money to buy power, while in the Middle East one uses power to acquire money. That is obviously an oversimplification, and there are significant exceptions on both sides. The misuse of public office for financial gain is not unknown in the United States; the use of money to buy into the political process is not unfamiliar in the traditional Middle East. But these are marginal, in the main small-scale, departures from the norm. In the vast American political and economic system the money made through the actual exercise of power is relatively unimportant—no more than small-time peculation. In the Middle East money can buy only the power of intrigue, not of command.

Perhaps the most striking manifestation of this difference between the two systems is in the merchant class and its place in the society and polity. Muslim societies, both medieval and early modern, often included a rich and varied industrial and commercial life, and evolved a wealthy and cultivated merchant class. But with brief and insignificant exceptions—as, for example, in a disputed borderland between rival states or in an interregnum between the collapse of one regime and the consolidation of another—they were never able to match the achievement of the rising European bourgeoisie in the creation of the modern West.

One reason is that a large proportion of them were non-Muslims, principally Christians and Jews, and therefore precluded from any decisive role in the political process. But far more important was the chronic, permanent insecurity, the sequence of upheavals and invasions, the ever-present threat of expropriation or destruction.

These traditional obstacles to democracy have in many ways been reinforced by the processes of modernization and by recent developments in the region. As already observed, the power of the state to dominate and terrorize the people has been vastly increased by modern methods. The philosophy of authoritarian rule has been sharpened and strengthened by imported totalitarian ideologies, which have served a double purpose—to sanctify rulers and leaders and to fanaticize their subjects and followers. The so-called Islamic fundamentalists are no exception in this respect.

Self-criticism in the West—a procedure until recently rarely practiced and little understood in the Middle East—provided useful ammunition. This use of the West against itself is particularly striking among the fundamentalists. Western democracy for them is part of the hated West, and that hatred is central to the ideas by which they define themselves, as in the past the free world defined itself first against Nazism and then against communism.

The changes wrought by modernization are by no means entirely negative. Some, indeed, are extremely positive. One such improvement is the emancipation of women. Though this still has a long way to go before it reaches Western levels, irreversible changes have already taken place. These changes are indispensable: a society can hardly aspire realistically to create and operate free institutions as long as it keeps half its members in a state of permanent subordination and the other half see themselves as domestic autocrats. Economic and social development has also brought new economic and social elements of profound importance—a literate middle class, commercial, managerial, and professional, that is very different from the military, bureaucratic, and religious elites that between them dominated the old order. These new groups are creating their own associations and organizations, and modifying the law to accommodate them. They are an indispensable component of civil society—previously lacking, yet essential to any kind of democratic polity.

There are also older elements in the Islamic tradition, older factors in Middle Eastern history, that are not hostile to democracy and that, in favorable circumstances, could even help in its development. Of special importance among these is the classical Islamic concept of supreme sovereignty—elective, contractual, in a sense even consensual and revocable. The Islamic caliphate, as prescribed and regulated by the holy law, may be an autocracy; it is in no sense a despotism. According to Sunni doctrine, the caliph was to be elected by those qualified to make a choice. The electorate was never defined, nor was any procedure of election ever devised or operated, but the elective principle remains central to Sunni religious jurisprudence, and that is not unimportant.

Again according to Sunni doctrine, the relationship between the caliph and his subjects is contractual. The word *bay'a*, denoting the ceremony at the inauguration of a new caliph, is sometimes translated as "homage" or "allegiance." Such translations, though no doubt reflecting the facts, do not accurately represent the principle. The word comes from an Arabic root meaning "to barter," hence "to buy and to sell," and originally referring to the clasping or slapping of hands with which in ancient Arabia a deal was normally concluded. The *bay'a* was thus conceived as a contract by which the subjects undertook to obey and the caliph in return undertook to perform certain duties specified by the jurists. If a caliph failed in those duties—and Islamic history shows that this was by no means a purely theoretical point—he could, subject to certain conditions, be removed from office.

This doctrine marks one of the essential differences between Islamic and other autocracies. An Islamic ruler is not above the law. He is subject to it, no less than the humblest of his servants. If he commands something that is contrary to the law, the duty of obedience lapses and is replaced not by the right but by the duty of disobedience.

Muslim spokesmen, particularly those who sought to find Islamic roots for Western practices, made much of the Islamic principle of consultation, according to which a ruler should not make arbitrary decisions by himself but should act only after consulting with suitably qualified advisers. This principle rests on two somewhat enigmatic passages in the Quran and on a number of treatises, mainly by ulama and statesmen, urging consultation with ulama or with statesmen. This principle has never been institutionalized, nor even formulated in the treatises of the holy law, though naturally rulers have from time to time consulted with their senior officials, more particularly in Ottoman times.

Of far greater importance was the acceptance of pluralism in Islamic law and practice. Almost from the beginning the Islamic world has shown an astonishing diversity. Extending over three continents, it embraced a wide variety of races, creeds, and cultures, which lived side by side in reasonable if intermittent harmony. Sectarian strife and religious persecution are not unknown in Islamic history, but they are rare and atypical, and never reached the level of intensity of the great religious wars and persecutions in Christendom.

Traditional Islam has no doctrine of human rights, the very notion of which might seem an impiety. Only God has rights— human beings have duties. But in practice the duty owed by one human being to another—more specifically, by a ruler to his subjects—may amount to what Westerners would call a right,

particularly when the discharge of this duty is a requirement of
holy law.

TWO TEMPTATIONS

It may be—and has been—argued that these legal and religious
principles have scant effect. The doctrine of elective and contractual sovereignty has been tacitly ignored since the days of the
early caliphate. The supremacy of the law has been flouted.
Tolerance of pluralism and diversity has dwindled or disappeared
in an age of heightened religious, ethnic, and social tensions.
Consultation, as far as it ever existed, is restricted to the ruler
and his inner circle, while personal dignity has been degraded
by tyrants who feel that they must torture and humiliate, not
just kill, their opponents.

And yet, despite all these difficulties and obstacles, the democratic ideal is steadily gaining force in the region, and increasing
numbers of Arabs have come to the conclusion that it is the best,
perhaps the only, hope for the solution of their economic, social,
and political problems.

What can we in the democratic world do to encourage the
development of democracy in the Islamic Middle East—and
what should we do to avoid impeding or subverting it? There
are two temptations to which Western governments have all
too often succumbed, with damaging results. They might be
called the temptation of the right and the temptation of the
left. The temptation of the right is to accept, and even to
embrace, the most odious of dictatorships as long as they are
acquiescent in our own requirements, and as long as their policies seem to accord with the protection of our own national
interests. The spectacle of the great democracies of the West in
comfortable association with tyrants and dictators can only
discourage and demoralize the democratic opposition in these
countries.

The more insidious temptation, that of the left, is to press Muslim regimes for concessions on human rights and related matters. Since ruthless dictatorships are impervious to such pressures, and are indeed rarely subjected to them, the brunt of such well-intentioned intervention falls on the more moderate autocracies, which are often in the process of reforming themselves in a manner and at a pace determined by their own conditions and needs. The pressure for premature democratization can fatally weaken such regimes and lead to their overthrow, not by democratic opposition but by other forces that then proceed to establish a more ferocious and determined dictatorship.

All in all, considering the difficulties that Middle Eastern countries have inherited and the problems that they confront, the prospects for Middle Eastern democracy are not good. But they are better than they have ever been before. Most of these countries face grave economic problems. If they fail to cope with these problems, then the existing regimes, both dictatorial and authoritarian, are likely to be overthrown and replaced, probably by one variety or another of Islamic fundamentalists. It has been remarked in more than one country that the fundamentalists are popular because they are out of power and cannot be held responsible for the present troubles. If they acquired power, and with it responsibility, they would soon lose that popularity. But this would not matter to them, since once in power they would not need popularity to stay there, and would continue to govern—some with and some without oil revenues to mitigate the economic consequences of their methods. In time even the fundamentalist regimes, despite their ruthless hold on power, would be either transformed or overthrown, but by then they would have done immense, perhaps irreversible, damage to the cause of freedom.

But their victory is by no means inevitable. There is always the possibility that democrats may form governments, or governments learn democracy. The increasing desire for freedom, and the better understanding of what it means, are hopeful signs. Now that the Cold War has ended and the Middle East is no longer a battlefield for rival power blocs, the peoples of the Middle East have the chance—if they can take it—to make their own decisions and find their own solutions. No one else can do it for them. For the first time in centuries, the choice is their own.

FIVE

Free at Last?

The Arab World in the Twenty-first Century

A S THE TWENTIETH CENTURY DREW TO AN END, IT became clear that a major change was taking place in the countries of the Arab world. For almost 200 years, those lands had been ruled and dominated by European powers and before that by non-Arab Muslim regimes—chiefly the Ottoman Empire. After the departure of the last imperial rulers, the Arab world became a political battleground between the United States and the Soviet Union during the Cold War. That, too, ended with the collapse of the Soviet Union in 1991. Arab governments and Arab dynasties (royal or presidential) began taking over. Arab governments and, to a limited but growing extent, the Arab peoples were at last able to confront their own problems and compelled to accept responsibility for dealing with them.

Europe, long the primary source of interference and domination, no longer plays any significant role in the affairs of the Arab world. Given the enormous oil wealth enjoyed by some Arab rulers and the large and growing Arab and Muslim population in Europe, the key question today is, what role will Arabs play in European affairs? With the breakup of the Soviet Union,

Russia ceased to be a major factor in the Arab world. But because of its proximity, its resources, and its large Muslim population, Russia cannot afford to disregard the Middle East. Nor can the Middle East afford to disregard Russia.

The United States, unlike Europe, has continued to play a central role in the Arab world. During the Cold War, the United States' interest in the region lay chiefly in countering the growing Soviet influence, such as in Egypt and Syria. Since the end of the Cold War, U.S. troops have appeared occasionally in the region, either as part of joint peace missions (as in Lebanon in 1982–83) or to rescue or protect Arab governments from their neighboring enemies (as in Kuwait and Saudi Arabia in 1990–91). But many in the Arab world—and in the broader Islamic world—have seen these activities as blatant U.S. imperialism. According to this perception, the United States is simply the successor to the now-defunct French, British, and Soviet empires and their various Christian predecessors, carrying out yet another infidel effort to dominate the Islamic world.

Increasing U.S. involvement in the Middle East led to a series of attacks on U.S. government installations during the 1980s and 1990s. At first, Washington's response to the attacks was to withdraw. After the attacks on the U.S. marine barracks in Beirut in 1983 and on the U.S. component of a United Nations mission in Mogadishu in 1993, Washington pulled out its troops, made angry but vague declarations, and then launched missiles into remote and uninhabited places. Even the 1993 attack on the World Trade Center, in New York City, brought no serious rejoinder. These responses were seen by many as an expression of fear and weakness rather than moderation, and they encouraged hope among Islamist militants that they would eventually triumph. It was not until 9/11 that Washington felt compelled to respond with force, first in Afghanistan and then in Iraq, which were perceived as the sources of these attacks.

Other powers, both external and within the region, are playing increasingly active roles. Two neighboring non-Arab but predominantly Muslim countries, Iran and Turkey, have a long history of involvement in Arab affairs. Although the Turks, no doubt because of their past experience, have remained cautious and defensive, mainly concerned with a possible threat from Kurdish northern Iraq, the Iranians have become more active, especially since Iran's Islamic Revolution entered a new militant and expansionist phase. The broader Islamic world, free from outside control for the first time in centuries, is also naturally interested in events in the heartland of Islam. China and India, which will share or compete for primacy in Asia and elsewhere in the twenty-first century, are also taking an interest in the region.

THE CHALLENGE OF PEACE

The political landscape within the Arab world has also changed dramatically since the end of the Cold War. Pan-Arabism, which once played a central role in the region, has effectively come to an end. Of the many attempts to unite different Arab countries, all but one—the unification of North and South Yemen after they were briefly separated by an imperial intrusion—have failed. Since the death of Egyptian President Gamal Abdel Nasser, in 1970, no Arab leader has enjoyed much support outside his own country. Nor has any Arab head of state dared to submit his attainment or retention of power to the genuinely free choice of his own people.

At the same time, issues of national identity are becoming more significant. Non-Arab ethnic minorities—such as the Kurds in Iran, Iraq, and Turkey and the Berbers in North Africa— historically posed no major threat to central governments, and relations were generally good between Arabs and their non-Arab Muslim compatriots. But a new situation arose after the defeat of Saddam Hussein in the Persian Gulf War. The U.S. invasion of Iraq in 1991 had a strictly limited purpose: to liberate Kuwait. When this was accomplished, U.S. forces withdrew, leaving Saddam in control of his armed forces and free to massacre those of his subjects, notably Kurds and Shi'ites, who had responded to the U.S. appeal for rebellion. Saddam was left in power, but his control did not extend to a significant part of northern Iraq, where a local Kurdish regime in effect became an autonomous government. This region was largely, although not entirely, Kurdish and included most of the Kurdish regions of Iraq. For the first time in modern history, there was a Kurdish country with a Kurdish government—at least in practice, if not in theory. This posed problems not only for the government of Iraq but also for those of some neighboring countries with significant Kurdish populations, notably Turkey. (Because of the strong opposition of these neighbors, the creation of an independent Kurdish state in the future seems unlikely. But a Kurdish component of a federal Iraq is a serious possibility.)

Another major problem for the region is the Palestinian issue. The current situation is the direct result of the policy, endorsed by the League of Nations and later by the United Nations, to create a Jewish national home in Palestine. With rare exceptions, the Arabs of Palestine and the leading Arab regimes resisted this policy from the start. A succession of offers for a Palestinian state in Palestine were made—by the British mandate government in 1937, by the United Nations in 1947—but each time Palestinian leaders and Arab regimes refused the offer because it would have meant recognizing the existence of a Jewish state next door. The struggle between the new state of Israel and the Palestinians has continued for over six decades, sometimes in the form of battles between armies (as in 1948, 1956, 1967, and 1973) and more recently between Israeli citizens and groups that are variously described as freedom fighters or terrorists.

The modern peace process began when President Anwar al-Sadat, of Egypt, fearing that the growing Soviet presence in the region was a greater threat to Arab independence than Israel could ever constitute, made peace with Israel in 1979. He was followed in 1994 by King Hussein of Jordan and, less formally, by other Arab states that developed some commercial and quasi-diplomatic contacts with Israel. Dialogue between Israel and the Palestine Liberation Organization led to some measure of formal mutual recognition and, more significant, to a withdrawal of Israeli forces from parts of the West Bank and the Gaza Strip and the establishment of more or less autonomous Palestinian authorities in these places.

But the conflict continues. Important sections of the Palestinian movement have refused to recognize the negotiations or any agreements and are continuing the armed struggle. Even some of those who have signed agreements—notably Yasir Arafat—have later shown a curious ambivalence toward their implementation. From the international discourse in English and other European languages, it would seem that most of the Arab states and some members of the Palestinian leadership have resigned themselves to accepting Israel as a state. But the discourse in Arabic—in broadcasts, sermons, speeches, and school textbooks—is far less conciliatory, portraying Israel as an illegitimate invader that must be destroyed. If the conflict is about the size of Israel, then long and difficult negotiations can eventually resolve the problem. But if the conflict is about the existence of Israel, then serious negotiation is impossible. There is no compromise position between existence and nonexistence.

RUNNING ON EMPTY

The state of the region's economy, and the resulting social and political situation, is a source of increasing concern in the Arab world. For the time being, oil continues to provide enormous wealth, directly to some countries in the region and indirectly to others. But these vast sums of money are creating problems as well as benefits. For one thing, oil wealth has strengthened autocratic governments and inhibited democratic development. Oil-rich rulers have no need to levy taxes and therefore no need to satisfy elected representatives. (In the Arab world, the converse of a familiar dictum is true: No representation without taxation.)

In addition to strengthening autocracy, oil wealth has also inhibited economic development. Sooner or later, oil will be either exhausted or replaced as an energy source, and the wealth and power that it provides will come to an end. Some more farsighted Arab governments, aware of this eventuality, have begun to encourage and foster other kinds of economic development. Some of the Persian Gulf states are showing impressive expansion, especially in tourism and international finance. But the returns accruing from these sectors are still limited compared to the enormous wealth derived from oil.

Oil wealth has also led to the neglect or abandonment of other forms of gainful economic activity. From 2002 to 2006, a committee of Arab intellectuals, working under the auspices of the United Nations, produced a series of reports on human development in the Arab world. With devastating frankness, they reviewed the economic, social, and cultural conditions in the Arab world and compared them with those of other regions. Some of these comparisons—reinforced by data from other international sources—revealed an appalling pattern of neglect and underdevelopment.

Over the last quarter of a century, real GDP per capita has fallen throughout the Arab world. In 1999, the GDP of all the Arab countries combined stood at $531.2 billion, less than that of Spain. Today, the total non-oil exports of the entire Arab world (which has a population of approximately 300 million people) amount to less than those of Finland (a country of only 5 million inhabitants). Throughout the 1990s, exports from the region, 70 percent of which are oil or oil-related products, grew at a rate of 1.5 percent, far below the average global rate of 6 percent. The number of books translated every year into Arabic in the entire Arab world is one-fifth the number translated into Greek in Greece. And the number of books, both those in their original language and those translated, published per million people in the Arab world is very low compared with the figures for other regions. (Sub-Saharan Africa has a lower figure, but just barely.)

The situation regarding science and technology is as bad or worse. A striking example is the number of patents registered in the United States between 1980 and 2000: from Saudi Arabia, there were 171; from Egypt, 77; from Kuwait, 52; from the United Arab Emirates, 32; from Syria, 20; and from Jordan, 15—compared with 16,328 from South Korea and 7,652 from Israel. Out of six world regions, that comprising the Middle East and North Africa received the lowest freedom rating from Freedom House. The Arab countries also have the highest illiteracy rates and one of the lowest numbers of active research scientists with frequently cited articles. Only sub-Saharan Africa has a lower average standard of living.

Another shock came with the 2003 publication in China of a list of the 500 best universities in the world. The list did not include a single one of the more than 200 universities in the Arab countries. Since then, new rankings have appeared every year. The Arab universities remain absent, even from the relatively short list for the Asia-Pacific region. In an era of total and untrammeled independence for the Arab world, these failings can no longer be attributed to imperial oppressors or other foreign malefactors.

One of the most important social problems in the Arab world, as elsewhere in the Islamic world, is the condition of women. Women constitute slightly more than half the population, but in most Arab countries they have no political power. Some Muslim observers have seen in the depressed and downtrodden status of the female Arab population one of the main reasons for the underdevelopment of their society as compared with the advanced West and the rapidly developing East. Modern communications and travel are making these contrasts ever more visible. Some countries, such as Iraq and Tunisia, have made significant progress toward the emancipation of women by increasing opportunities for them. In Iraq, women have gained access to higher education and, consequently, to an ever-widening range of professions. In Tunisia, equal rights for women were guaranteed in the 1959 constitution. The results have been almost universal education for women and a significant number of women among the ranks of doctors, journalists, lawyers, magistrates, and teachers, as well as in the worlds of business and politics. This is perhaps the most hopeful single factor for the future of freedom and progress in these countries.

Another social problem is immigrant communities in the Arab world, which have received far less attention than Arab immigrant communities in Europe. These immigrants are attracted by oil wealth and the opportunities that it provides, and they undertake tasks that local people are either unwilling or unable to perform. This is giving rise to new and growing alien communities in several Arab countries, such as South Asians in the United Arab Emirates. The assimilation of immigrants from one Arab country into another has often proved difficult, and the acceptance of non-Arab and non-Muslim immigrants from remoter lands poses a more serious problem.

All these problems are aggravated by the communications revolution, which is having an enormous impact on the Arab population across all social classes. Even in premodern times, government control of news and ideas in the Islamic countries was limited—the mosque, the pulpit, and, above all, the pilgrimage provided opportunities for the circulation of both information and ideas without parallel in the Western world. To some extent, modern Middle Eastern governments had learned how to manipulate information, but that control is rapidly diminishing as modern communications technology, such as satellite television and the Internet, has made people in the Arab countries, as elsewhere, keenly aware of the contrasts between different groups in their own countries and, more important, of the striking differences between the situations in their countries and those in other parts of the world. This has led to a great deal of anger and resentment, often directed against the West, as well as a countercurrent striving for democratic reform.

THE RISE OF THE RADICALS

Most Westerners saw the defeat and collapse of the Soviet Union as a victory in the Cold War. For many Muslims, it was nothing of the sort. In some parts of the Islamic world, the collapse of the Soviet Union represented the devastating loss of a patron that was difficult or impossible to replace. In others, it symbolized the defeat of an enemy and a victory for the Muslim warriors who forced the Soviets to withdraw from Afghanistan. As this latter group saw it, the millennial struggle between the true believers and the unbelievers had gone through many phases, during which the Muslims were led by various lines of caliphs and the unbelievers by various infidel empires. During the Cold War, the leadership of the unbelievers was contested between two rival superpowers, the United States and the Soviet Union. Since they—the Muslim holy warriors in Afghanistan—had disposed of the larger, fiercer, and more dangerous of the two in the 1980s, dealing with the other, they believed, would be comparatively easy.

That task was given a new urgency by the two U.S. interventions in Iraq: that during the brief Persian Gulf War of 1990–91 and the 2003 invasion that resulted in the overthrow of Saddam and the attempt to create a new and more democratic political and social order. Opinions differ on the measure of U.S. achievements so far, but even its limited success has been sufficient to cause serious alarm, both to regimes with a vested interest in the survival of the existing order and, more important, to groups with their own radical plans for overthrowing it.

In the eyes of Islamist radicals, both of these wars have constituted humiliating defeats for Islam at the hands of the surviving infidel superpower. This point has been made with particular emphasis by Osama bin Ladin, a Saudi who played a significant role in the war against the Soviets in Afghanistan and subsequently emerged as a very articulate leader in the Islamic world and as the head of al Qā'ida, a new Islamist radical group. He has repeatedly made his case against the United States, most notably in his declaration of jihad of February 1998, in which he elaborated three grievances against the infidel enemies of Islam. The first was the presence of U.S. troops in Saudi Arabia, the holy land of Islam. The second was the use of Saudi bases for an attack on Iraq, the seat of the longest and most glorious period of classical Islamic history. The third was U.S. support for the seizure of Jerusalem by what he contemptuously called "the statelet" (*duwayla*) of the Jews.

Another claimant for the mantle of Islamic leadership is the Islamic Republic of Iran. The 1979 Iranian Revolution constituted a major shift in power, with a major ideological basis, and had a profound impact across the Muslim world. Its influence was by no means limited to Shi'ite communities. It was also very extensive and powerful in countries where there is little or no Shi'ite presence and where Sunni-Shi'ite differences therefore have little political or emotional significance. The impact of the Iranian Revolution in the Arab countries was somewhat delayed because of the long and bitter Iran-Iraq War (1980–88), but from the end of the war onward, Iran's influence began to grow, particularly among Shi'ites in neighboring Arab countries. These populations, even in those places where they are numerous, had for centuries lived under what might be described as a Sunni ascendancy. The Iranian Revolution, followed by the regime change in Iraq in 2003, gave them new hope; the Shi'ite struggle has once again, for the first time in centuries, become a major theme of Arab politics. This struggle is very important where Shi'ites constitute a majority of the population (as in Iraq) or a significant proportion of the population (as in Lebanon, Syria, and parts of the eastern and southern Arabian Peninsula). For some time now, the eastern Arab world has seen the odd spectacle of Sunni and Shi'ite extremists occasionally cooperating in the struggle against the infidels while continuing their internal struggle against one another. (One example of this is Iran's support for both the strongly Sunni Hamas in Gaza and the strongly Shi'ite Hezbollah in Lebanon.)

The increasing involvement of Iran in the affairs of the Arab world has brought about major changes. First, Iran has developed into a major regional power, its influence extending to Lebanon and the Palestinian territories. Second, although the rift between the Sunnis and the Shi'ites is significant, Iran's involvement has rendered it less important than the divide between both of them and their non-Arab, non-Muslim enemies. Third, just as the perceived Soviet threat induced Sadat to make peace with Israel in 1979, today some Arab leaders see the threat from Iran as more dangerous than that posed by Israel and therefore are quietly seeking accommodation with the Jewish state. During the 2006 war between Israeli forces and Hezbollah, the usual pan-Arab support for the Arab side was replaced by a cautious, even expectant, neutrality. This realignment may raise some hope for Arab-Israeli peace.

THE STRUGGLE FOR THE FUTURE

For much of the twentieth century, two imported Western ideologies dominated in the Arab world: socialism and nationalism. By the beginning of the twenty-first century, these worldviews had become discredited. Both had, in effect, accomplished the reverse of their declared aims. Socialist plans and projects were put in place, but they did not bring prosperity. National independence was achieved, but it did not bring freedom; rather, it allowed foreign overlords to be replaced with domestic tyrants, who were less inhibited and more intimate in their tyranny. Another imported European model, the one-party ideological dictatorship, brought neither prosperity nor dignity—only tyranny sustained by indoctrination and repression.

Today, most Arab regimes belong to one of two categories: those that depend on the people's loyalty and those that depend on their obedience. Loyalty may be ethnic, tribal, regional, or some combination of these; the most obvious examples of systems that rely on loyalty are the older monarchies, such as those of Morocco and the Arabian Peninsula. The regimes that depend on obedience are European-style dictatorships that use techniques of control and enforcement derived from the fascist and communist models. These regimes have little or no claim to the loyalty of their people and depend for survival on diversion and repression: directing the anger of their people toward some external enemy—such as Israel, whose misdeeds are a universally sanctioned public grievance—and suppressing discontent with ruthless police methods. In those Arab countries where the government depends on force rather than loyalty, there is clear evidence of deep and widespread discontent, directed primarily against the regime and then inevitably against those who are seen to support it. This leads to a paradox—namely, that countries with pro-Western regimes usually have anti-Western populations, whereas the populations of countries with anti-Western regimes tend to look to the West for liberation.

Both of these models are becoming less effective; there are groups, increasing in number and importance, that seek a new form of government based not primarily on loyalty, and still less on repression, but on consent and participation. These groups are still small and, of necessity, quiet, but the fact that they have appeared at all is a remarkable development. Some Arab states have even begun to experiment, cautiously, with elected assemblies formed after authentically contested elections, notably Iraq after its 2005 election.

In some countries, democratic opposition forces are growing, but they are often vehemently anti-Western. The recent successes of Hamas and Hezbollah demonstrate that opposition parties can fare very well when their critiques are cast in religious, rather than political, terms. The religious opposition parties have several obvious advantages. They express both their critiques and their aspirations in terms that are culturally familiar and easily accepted, unlike those of Western-style democrats. In the mosques, they have access to a communications network—and therefore tools to disseminate propaganda—unparalleled in any other sector of the community. They are relatively free from corruption and have a record of helping the suffering urban masses. A further advantage, compared with secular democratic opposition groups, is that whereas the latter are required by their own ideologies to tolerate the propaganda of their opponents, the religious parties have no such obligation. Rather, it is their sacred duty to suppress and crush what they see as antireligious, anti-Islamic movements. Defenders of the existing regimes argue, not implausibly, that loosening the reins of authority would lead to a takeover by radical Islamist forces.

Lebanon is the one country in the entire region with a significant experience of democratic political life. It has suffered not for its faults but for its merits—the freedom and openness that others have exploited with devastating effect. More recently, there have been some hopeful signs that the outside exploitation and manipulation of Lebanon might at last be diminishing. The Palestinian leadership has been gone for decades; Syria was finally induced to withdraw its forces in 2005, leaving the Lebanese, for the first time in decades, relatively free to conduct their own affairs. Indeed, the Cedar Revolution of 2005 was seen as the beginning of a new era for Lebanon. But Lebanese democracy is far from secure. Syria retains a strong interest in the country, and Hezbollah—trained, armed, and financed by Iran—has become increasingly powerful. There have been some signs of a restoration of Lebanese stability and democracy, but the battle is not yet over, nor will it be, until the struggle for democracy spreads beyond the borders of Lebanon.

Today, there are two competing diagnoses of the ills of the region, each with its own appropriate prescription. According to one, the trouble is all due to infidels and their local dupes and imitators. The remedy is to resume the millennial struggle against the infidels in the West and return to God-given laws and traditions. According to the other diagnosis, it is the old ways, now degenerate and corrupt, that are crippling the Arab world. The cure is openness and freedom in the economy, society, and the state—in a word, genuine democracy. But the road to democracy—and to freedom—is long and difficult, with many obstacles along the way. It is there, however, and there are some visionary leaders who are trying to follow it. At the moment, both Islamic theocracy and liberal democracy are represented in the region. The future place of the Arab world in history will depend, in no small measure, on the outcome of the struggle between them.

SIX

Gender and the Clash of Civilizations

L ET ME BEGIN WITH A QUOTATION FROM AN Ottoman writer called Selaniki Mustafa Efendi who was a high public official in the Ottoman administration and also doubled as what in the Ottoman system was called the Vakanüvis (the chronicler of events). It was his job, among others, to keep a record of important public events. On the date of the Muslim calendar corresponding to October 1593, Selaniki Mustafa Efendi recorded, among the notable events of the month, the arrival in Istanbul of an English ambassador. The ambassador seems to have interested him very little; he has nothing whatever to say about him. He does talk quite a lot about the ship in which the ambassador arrived, which certainly drew his attention—a vessel built for the Atlantic and (he notes with horror) carrying more than eighty guns. But that's not what concerns us this evening. The other extraordinary thing about the arrival of this English ambassador was the monarch who sent him: he is sent, he says, by a woman—the ruler of the Island of England is a woman—and one can almost read the astonishment in the lines of the chronicle: "A woman who rules her inherited realm with complete power." Now he wasn't quite right about that: Elizabeth did have to contend with elected parliaments, but that would have been even more unintelligible to him. Reigning queens were not entirely outside the experience of Muslim history and civilization, and therefore Muslim historians. They did occasionally hear about them, sometimes even in quite early times. They knew, for example, of the Empress Irene in Byzantium. If you look at Qalqashandī, who in the fourteenth century put together a kind of manual of bureaucratic protocol, he mentions a certain Joan, Queen of Naples, and sets forth the titles to be used in addressing her, naturally feminine in form. And he ends by saying: "When she is replaced by a man, the titles may be used in the masculine form, or more exalted titles, given the superiority of men over women." Even in Ottoman times, they were not entirely unacquainted with queens: Elizabeth and other queens of England; Maria Theresa of Austria, Catherine of Russia, Isabella of Spain, and so on. The phenomenon was not unknown, and it did not always arouse the same consternation—I think that is the right word.

Now we use the word *queen* in English and in other Western languages in two different senses: there is the queen who reigns, who succeeds to the throne and is in every sense the monarch, the sovereign. We also use the word *queen* in another sense, to denote the consort of the king. If there is a king and he has a wife, that wife is queen. This is normal in European and even some non-European monarchies. In the Muslim world, this was totally unknown and would have been incomprehensible. In that sense, they had no queens; they knew of no queens. Muslim sovereigns—caliphs, sultans, and others—did not have a consort; they had a harem. And this gave rise to an entirely different situation.

Here we may look at the pattern of public life as far as it is known to us. In the earlier periods, both of the Arab caliphate and of the Ottoman sultanate, we do know something about the ladies of the court. We are told about marriages that were arranged between a prince of the reigning dynasty and a lady of some other dynasty or some other distinguished family. We are even given some information about the mothers of the sultans or the caliphs in earlier times. But that passed very rapidly, in both cases. For most of their recorded history, there was no queen, no established consort, only a harem consisting mainly of slave concubines. After the earliest period, the sultans and the caliphs were mostly born to slave mothers, for the most part of unknown background.

Women in the court could achieve significance, but not as wives. They could achieve major significance as mothers: the mother of the reigning sultan had the title *valide sultan*, which could be an important position with some possibility of exercising influence. The daughters of the sultan were also given a certain status: they were even allowed to use the word *sultan* after, not before their names. And anyone who had the misfortune to marry one of these ladies was given the title *damad*—a Persian word meaning "son-in-law," which became a title. I say misfortune because the evidence that we have shows that being an imperial son-in-law was, to say the least, a dubious privilege, often leading to considerable tensions between the natural superiority of the husband in a Muslim household and the artificial superiority claimed for merely being the daughter of the reigning sultan.

If you compare the history of the Abbasids, the Ottomans, and other great dynasties in the history of Islam with those of Europe, you will immediately be struck by this almost total absence of women. In the history of the European dynasties, without exception, women play an important part: pedigrees cover both sides; royal marriages and intermarriages are an important part of the political process—and, of course, at certain periods, royal mistresses.

In the Middle East and elsewhere in the Islamic world, the feminine element is almost entirely missing from historiography.

This, of course, has a devastating effect on another art closely associated with historiography—namely, biography. And that is perhaps one reason (I will not say it is the only reason, it may not even be the main reason, but I think it is an important reason) that although Islamic literature is immensely rich in historiographic writings, it is correspondingly poor in biographical writings. We have vast numbers of short biographies, running to a few lines or at the most a couple of pages, in biographical dictionaries (an art form that was probably invented in the Islamic world) grouped together by profession or vocation or by some other factor. But we have very few biographies of individuals. Whereas for the European monarchies, from quite an early date, we find book-length biographies of this or that or the other king or queen or prince or princess, very few of the rulers of Islam were ever given that honor. And perhaps one reason for this lack is the difficulty of writing half a biography, so to speak.

Let me turn now to the larger question of the place of women in this society, not just at the top in the reigning family but more generally. And here I must begin with a historian's adaptation of a famous American question: what do we know, and when did we know it? I would add, of course—how do we know it, and what are our sources of information?

Obviously, in the first place, there are the usual literary sources: the chronicles and other literary works, and these, as I have remarked, tell us remarkably little about the feminine element at court or anywhere else. We do know of a few remarkable women who, in times of crisis, by force of personality, managed to play a role, but this is usually brief, exceptional, and normally regarded by the chroniclers with strong disapproval. We have rather more, but still not a great deal, in literary history, where we are told of the occasional appearance of women poets, but again, there are very few, and they appear only at certain periods and then disappear.

Much more informative on this subject is the religious and legal literature, the two of course, in Islam as in Judaism, being intimately interconnected; starting with the Quran itself, the biography of the Prophet, the traditions of the Prophet, and the immense literature of commentary and explanation arising out of them. These constitute our first and most basic source of information about the position of women in society, and the position that emerges from them is, I think, sufficiently well known. According to Quranic legislation, a man may marry up to four wives and have as many slave concubines as he can afford. The formula is "those whom your right hand owns." This is generally understood to mean slaves who are owned by a man. And it is a principle of law, as it was also in biblical antiquity, that the male owner of a female slave is allowed full sexual rights over her. The female owner of a male slave has no such privileges, though it is possible for a free woman to own a male slave.

In addition to the literary evidence, we also have rich documentary evidence. This is of particular importance in dealing with this subject. This is a region where we still have vast archives full of masses of information that have so far still been very imperfectly explored, and for gender studies in Islamic civilization, some of these are of particular relevance. One is inheritance: Islamic law regulates very precisely the shares that heirs are to receive from the estate of the deceased. It is not like the Anglo-American system, where one can make a will disposing more or less freely of one's assets. This is not the Islamic law; the law lays down with great precision what goes to sons, to daughters, to nephews and nieces, in what proportions, and so on. To enforce this law, it was necessary to compile inventories of the estates of deceased persons, and there was a public official whose duty it was to supervise the preparation of these inventories and the distribution of the assets in accordance with the Shariʿa. Thanks to this, we have literally hundreds of thousands of such documents: inventories of the estates of deceased persons with instructions for how they should be distributed. And this is a priceless source of economic, social, and also cultural information on life in the times and places from which these records come.

Another is the Waqf records: a Waqf, I should explain, is a pious foundation, a deed establishing what in modern language would be called a trust, by which the doner, male or female, donates certain assets that are then to be used for purposes specified in the Waqf document. We have again vast numbers of these records: Waqf registers with very full details of who established them; how, when, and in what circumstances; what are the assets and income; and how they are to be used. This again is a rich and priceless source of information.

A third documentary source is what are called the Sijills: these are the records of matters that are brought before the Qadi, the local judge, for adjudication. The case is brought before him and is recorded; the evidence and the decision are recorded.

From all these, we can build up a picture of the position of women in Muslim society that is vastly more detailed and, I suppose one must also add, vastly more reliable than what one would gather from the literary and juridical evidence. Certain interesting things appear: it has often been remarked that the position of women in the Islamic world was in one important respect significantly better than that of women in the Western world until quite modern times. That is in the ownership of property. In the Western world, until fairly recently, in most countries married women did not dispose of their own property, which became more or less the property of, or at least was fully controlled by, the husband. This was not the case in Islamic law. A woman could own property, inherit property, and even after marriage, retain certain rights to the property she brought into the marriage. If she was divorced by her husband without proper reason, she was entitled to full restitution of any part of her property that had been consumed. This is a very important aspect: we can see this; it is not just an abstract legal principle. We see it very fully documented in the inheritance registers and in the Waqf registers: a remarkably high proportion of these Waqfs were established by women of property who chose this way of establishing a trust, often for the benefit of their heirs.

Now what sort of pattern of social life emerges from this? The basic pattern of marriage is one of polygamy and concubinage. We have a curious situation in the Ottoman Empire where the different *millets* lived side by side, each permitted by the Ottoman system to enforce (and I use the word *enforce* advisedly) its own laws, still under the supreme sovereignty of the Ottoman state. On the question of women, Muslims, Christians, and Jews differed quite significantly. Muslims were allowed both polygamy and concubinage; Christians were allowed neither; Jews were allowed polygamy but not concubinage; in antiquity, Jews used both, but by medieval and early modern times, concubinage had been ruled out by the rabbinate but polygamy was still permitted among Jewish communities in Islamic countries and remains so to the present day. It was prohibited by the rabbis in Christendom.

Here we have, then, three different communities living side by side with three different rules regarding marriage: among the Christians, strict monogamy—legally, that is. I am not prepared to issue any guarantees as to what actually happened, but polygamy was forbidden and concubinage was forbidden in all forms of Christianity. For Jews, polygamy, yes; concubinage, no. However, if we look at the tombstones in Jewish cemeteries, we will find a large number of women whose pedigree is given as *Bat Avraham Avinu*, "Daughter of our father Abraham," clearly meaning a convert, and this usually means a bought slave used as a concubine against rabbinic law, and therefore converted and married to make it legal.

Another very important source of information is travel: people traveling to and from the Islamic world and, more particularly, between the Islamic world and Christian Europe. The material from travelers from west to east is much more voluminous and much more detailed than from east to west. There were always many travelers who went from west to east; they had many reasons for doing so. They had religious reasons—the Christian and Jewish holy places were under Muslim rule, and if they wanted to go on a pilgrimage to their holy places, they had to go to Muslim countries. Muslims had no holy places in Christendom; their holy places were safely under Muslim rule, and they therefore needed to go on no pilgrimages abroad.

During the periods of Muslim efflorescence, commerce was a very powerful motivation, bringing Christians and Jews from Europe into the Islamic lands. Diplomacy also sent Europeans abroad. The European states, as soon as it became possible, extended the European practice of establishing resident embassies and consulates to Muslim as well as European cities. The Muslims did no such thing; they regarded this as an absurd waste of time and money. If they had something to say, they sent an ambassador; he said it and, having said it, he returned home. We do not find Muslim resident embassies or consulates until the end of the eighteenth century, when they begin to adopt European ways, and the practice did not really get going until toward the middle of the nineteenth century.

The travel documentation from the Muslim side is therefore comparatively poor; it consists basically of two groups: diplomats who were sent on these special missions for a limited time and a limited purpose, and members of their embassies; and prisoners, people who were taken captive and somehow managed to be ransomed or escape and who returned home. But even they are remarkably few and remarkably limited. They do, however, give us an interesting spectrum of Muslim reactions to what they found in Christendom, and a little later, I intend to offer you some samples of these.

Among Western visitors to the Middle East, there were women from quite an early date. Some went as wives of merchants or ambassadors, the most notable being an English woman, Lady Mary Wortley Montagu, whose letters from Turkey are some of the most enlightening documents on that topic. Later, there were some vigorous spinsters who went on their own travel and adventures, in the Middle East and elsewhere.

From the east to the west—almost zero. Muslim women did not travel abroad; when their men went, if they took women at all, they were hidden away in the harem in the women's quarters, for which special arrangements were made during long journeys. And even if they had anything to say, they probably would not have been able to say it, lacking the education necessary for that purpose. So until comparatively modern times, until the rise of feminism in the Muslim east, the beginnings of female education, and consequently of female travel, we have virtually total silence from Muslim women dealing with the West. When it begins, it becomes very active and very interesting and, of course, continues to the present day.

How do they react to each other? In very mixed ways. A good deal of what we find on both sides can only be described as fantasy. Given the nature of Muslim domestic life, European visitors had very little opportunity of finding out anything or even of talking to anybody who knew anything and was willing to tell. So a large part of what we find in the Western travel literature consists of fantasy, gossip, hearsay, rumor, and the like—often quite interesting in itself but more interesting for what it tells us about the visitors than about the places they visited. Western males often talk with ill-concealed envy of what they imagine to be the rights and privileges of the Muslim male. Muslim visitors to Europe, on the other hand, speak with horror and disgust of what they see as the free and easy ways of Western women and the promiscuous and totally sinful way of life of men and women alike. A point frequently made by Muslim travelers is the lack of manly jealousy on the part of Western males; they are constantly astonished at the kind of things that Western husbands are prepared to put up with, without apparently seeing anything wrong in them.

This begins quite early: we find it, for example, among Arab contemporary writers of the period of the Crusades who sometimes managed to visit Crusaders socially during intervals of peace; they express astonishment at the way women are treated and behave in Crusader circles.

Let me come back to the question of information: one branch of literature that is of some interest is what one might call "consumer reports." We know that a large part of the female population consisted of slaves; there were also male slaves, of course, but they are not our present concern. From quite an early date, we find reports for the guidance of purchasers of slaves, describing the different kinds of slaves, what they are good for, what are their qualities, and what are their defects.

Normally, the classification is ethnic. Under Muslim law, it was forbidden to enslave a free person, Muslim or non-Muslim, within the Islamic lands. Slaves could become slaves by birth—that is, being born to slave parents—by capture, or by importation; in other words, they were either captured in the jihad, in which case it was lawful to enslave them, or they were enslaved already before they entered Muslim lands. This meant that the overwhelming majority of the slave population came from outside, from Asia, from Africa, and for quite a long time, from Europe.

So the slave trader's vade mecums—or, one might say, the slave buyer's consumer guides—deal with them mainly by ethnicity and describe the different qualities of different ethnicities of slaves and what they're useful for. This also gives us some information about what they were used for, apart from the obvious ones. These begin at quite an early date and continue until almost modern times. One fairly recent one is by a certain

Fazil Bey, who was a minor official in the Ottoman court at the end of the eighteenth century. He was Palestinian by origin, the grandson of the famous Dāhir al-ʿUmar of Safed. When Dāhir al-ʿUmar, who was a rebel against the Ottomans, was suppressed, the Ottomans, in accordance with their common practice, took his family to Istanbul and tried to convert them into loyal servants of the Ottoman dynasty. Fazil Bey was born and brought up in Istanbul and was a minor poet; he wrote two books that are very relevant to our topic. One of them is the *Zenānnāme*, "The Book of Women." It is not unreasonable to call it a consumers' guide to women by nationality: what they are good for, what they are less good for, which are preferable, and so on. He includes all the different ethnic groups within the Ottoman Empire since, remember, he is not talking about slaves this time, he is talking about women, including free women, and therefore the domestic population is also covered. He also includes women from outside the Ottoman Empire and has a fairly detailed study of various European nationalities with some appropriate (or some may think inappropriate) comments on each. Sometimes one wonders how he got his information: speaking of women from the Netherlands, for example, he says, "They speak a difficult language and are without sexual attraction." One wonders what brought him to either of these conclusions.

He notes that Spanish women are good at playing the guitar. This book has never been published; there are, to my knowledge, two excellent manuscripts, one in the University of Istanbul Library and the other in the British Museum. Both are richly illustrated with contemporary miniatures. Fazil Bey's consumers' guide to women was accompanied by a second one called *The Book of Boys*. But that brings up another topic, to which I will return later.

I did mention Fazil Bey's illustrations. We have a certain number of pictures, but on the whole, they are not terribly helpful to the historian since they did not go in very much for realistic portraiture, and what we do have is mostly male, not female, apart from Fazil Bey's book.

I have been talking about evidence—literary evidence, historical evidence, documentary evidence, archival evidence, and others. What about reality, the observed reality as we see it now, as well as what European observers have been recording for some time past now? Here we find a number of rather striking contrasts between the familiar observed reality of the Muslim world at the present time and the traditional picture as embodied in the law and in tradition. For example, a vexed question is that of female circumcision, also called excision, which is regarded in many parts of the Islamic world as a basic principle of Islam. It is nothing of the kind: it is totally absent from the Qur'ān, from reliable hadiths, and from early Sharī'a textbooks. It is obviously a local custom of some parts of what became the world of Islam, which, like many other local customs, was, so to speak, Islamized and given an Islamic coloring. It is not part of Islam and is by no means universal in the Islamic world. Another custom of which we are acutely conscious in present times is what is quaintly called "honor killing." Here again, there is a striking difference between practice and the law. The Sharī'a certainly strongly condemns adultery, but the Sharī'a goes to quite elaborate lengths to make sure that women are not murdered on false charges of adultery. Rather than go through the complicated procedures of divorce, which might also involve some restoration of property, it is quicker, cheaper, and more expeditious to accuse one's wife of adultery and then summarily dispose of her while retaining her assets. It is no doubt to prevent this that the jurists insist on the most elaborate proof. A charge of adultery must be verified by four adult male witnesses; obviously, it would be a singularly incompetent adulterer who would allow that to happen. In fact, these are dispensed with or may easily be purchased for a modest sum from a group who are known as professional witnesses. This is a second point, after excision, where there is a striking contrast between common practice and what perhaps a non-Muslim may be permitted to call authentic Islam.

A third difference, the other way round, is on the question of homosexuality. There are two kinds: the kind that in Arabic is called *Liwāt*, from Lot, meaning male homosexuality, and the kind called *Sihāk*, which is female homosexuality or lesbianism. Islam, like Judaism and like Christianity, totally forbids any kind of homosexual encounter. But the climate of opinion, if I may call it that, was in the past on the whole much more tolerant of male homosexuality, to such a degree that in many times and places it was virtually open and unconcealed. Fazil Bey, whom I mentioned earlier, wrote his book on women, and then he wrote a book on boys—the two side by side. One gets the impression that he was more interested in women than in boys, since the one on women is more detailed and more interesting. The one on boys, one feels, he wrote because the public demanded it. There are others—poets, for example—who have separate sections in their divans for love poems addressed to women and love poems addressed to boys. In the main literary tradition, there is virtually no attempt to conceal male homosexuality, which, although contrary to the Holy Law, is nevertheless very much regarded as part of life at the court and everywhere else. There the tolerance of homosexuality was almost total. It is also a point raised by some Muslim visitors to Europe, who get very angry at the European assumption that all Muslims are homosexuals and that that is their normal activity. Modern Islamist movements have adopted a much more severe condemnation of homosexuality in all its forms.

Regarding female homosexuality, for obvious reasons, the evidence is scantier and more difficult to obtain. One assumes that where large numbers of women are confined in one place, sharing one husband with only the eunuchs to attend them, it would have been a natural consequence. The European travelers have some rather piquant details on this subject.

I have already mentioned the question of what women do. Obviously, their primary function is sex and motherhood, and this is very clear from the slave literature and other sources. But they did also have other tasks—the obvious domestic tasks of wives and mothers, of bringing up children, running the household, and the like. But here I would note that until fairly recent times, cooking and serving meals was not so central a part of wifehood as it has been in the Western world. Many town dwellers got their meals from the various people who prepared and sold different kinds of foodstuffs in the markets, a point commented on by a number of travelers.

As far as gainful employment is concerned, information is scattered and limited. There does seem to have been some but not a great deal. One area where we do find women playing a rather prominent role is in what, for want of a better term, we might call entertainment: dancing, singing, reciting poetry, even composing poetry for occasions. This obviously required a certain level of education and sophistication. The entertainers were normally slaves, talented slaves, trained under the auspices of their owners and used by them for the entertainment of their guests.

Let me come now to my final topic, the impact of modernity—how did the encounter with the Western world, on a much larger scale than before, affect the position of women in this society? As long as it was simply a matter of odd individual visitors going one way or the other, the two could remain almost hermetically sealed. But in modern times that ceased to be possible, and roughly from the end of the eighteenth century onward, we get closer and closer contact between the two rival civilizations, Christendom and Islam, and therefore more and more awareness of this really crucial difference between the two.

I would like to quote a few examples: they are by no means all one way. One of the most interesting writers from the East is a man from Lahore in what is now Pakistan and was then India, a man of Persian background, who visited Western Europe at the end of the eighteenth century and the beginning of the nineteenth century. His name is Mirza Abü Ṭālib Khan, and his book is called *Masīr-i Ṭālibī* (in Persian)—a fascinating work in which he describes in considerable detail what he found in England, in Ireland, and in France, which were the countries he visited. He—as far as I know—is quite alone in saying that men in England have far greater control over their women than do Muslims, because they don't wear veils and they don't cover their faces; their husbands can always know where they are going, and they can't go off to secret assignations on the pretense of visiting neighbors or friends or cousins. Also, he notes, their husbands actually put them to work, to keep them busy and gainfully employed.

Abü Ṭālib Khan's observations are interesting but, as far as I know, unique. Generally, comments are quite the other way round: expressing shock and horror. The first time Muslims really had close contact with Westerners in large numbers was the French expedition to Egypt at the end of the eighteenth and beginning of the nineteenth century. Now, for the first time, there were large numbers of Frenchmen with their wives and families, living in a Muslim city—close up, so to speak—and if we look at Jabartī, the Egyptian historian of that time, we find expressions of shock, horror, and above all disgust with the way that Westerners conducted their lives, particularly their social relations. Shaykh Rifā'a Rafi' al-Ṭahtāwī, who spent a few years in Paris as tutor to the first Egyptian student mission, has some interesting quotes.

But then, from about the 1860s onward, we get a totally different approach. Namık Kemal, one of the Young Ottomans, in an article published in 1867, first put forward the idea that the backwardness (he did not have to worry about political correctness in those days; he could use such words freely) of their society

compared with the West "is due to the way we treat our women."
He makes a very simple point: if we deprive ourselves of the
talents and services of half the population, how can we hope to
keep up with the Western world? And he uses a very striking
image: compared with the West, our society is like a human
body that is paralyzed on one side.

From then onward, there are feminist movements—some
among women, some among men—and this becomes a significant factor. There is also a significant reaction against it: it
becomes a major point in the polemic against the West, against
Westernization, and against Westernizing Middle Eastern rulers.
And here I will quote just a few examples: Sayyid Qutb, one of
the ideological leaders of the Muslim Brothers, was an Egyptian
teacher and, later, a Ministry of Education official who spent just
under two years in the United States between 1948 and 1950 and
wrote with utter shock and horror of the dreadful things he
found there. In America, he says, everything, even religion, is
measured in material terms, by size, by bigness, by numbers.
There are many churches, but this should not mislead you into
thinking that there is any real religion or any real spiritual
feeling. For the minister of a church, as for the manager of a
business or a theater, success is what matters, and to achieve
success, they advertise and offer what Americans most seek: a
good time or fun. The text is in Arabic but he writes "a good
time" and "fun" in English in the Arabic text. "The result," he
says "is that even Church recreation halls, with the blessing of
the priesthood, hold dances where people of both sexes meet,
mix and touch." One can almost sense his shock and horror
when he says the ministers even go so far as to dim the lights in
order to facilitate the proceedings of the dance. Here I quote
directly: "The dance is inflamed by the notes of the gramo-
phone, the dance hall becomes a whirl of heels and thighs, arms
enfold hips, lips and breasts meet and the air is full of lust." He
then goes on to quote the Kinsey report, which had just been

published at that time. This and similar descriptions of dance halls may perhaps help us understand why these are regarded as legitimate targets for terrorist attack; it is a theme that comes up again and again and again.

On the lack of manly virility, here is a quotation from a Moroccan ambassador in Spain in 1766—Spain, remember. He says their dwellings have windows overlooking the street where the women sit all the time greeting the passersby. Their husbands treat them with the greatest courtesy; the women are very much addicted to conversational conviviality with men other than their husbands, in company and in private. They are not restrained from going wherever they wish; it often happens that a Christian returns to his home and finds his wife or his daughter or his sister in the company of another Christian, a stranger, drinking together and leaning against each other. He is delighted with this, and according to what I am told, he esteems it as a favor from the Christian who is in the company of his wife or whichever other woman of his household it may be. This is in Spain, of all places!

At the end of some further description of this, he says, after describing one of these receptions: "When the party dispersed, we returned to our lodgings and we prayed to God to save us from the wretched state of these Infidels who are devoid of manly jealousy and are sunk in unbelief and we implore the Almighty not to hold us accountable for our offense in conversing with them as circumstances required."

Another Ottoman ambassador at about the same time, Mehmed Efendi, who served in Paris, says, "In France, women are of a higher station than men, so they do what they wish and go where they please, and the greatest lord shows respect and courtesy beyond all limits to the humblest of women. In that country, their commands prevail. It is said that France is the paradise of women where they have no cares or troubles and where whatever they desire is theirs without effort."

Shaykh Rifāʻa, mentioned earlier, was in Paris between 1826 and 1831. He says, "Men among them are the slaves of women and subject to their commands, whether they be beautiful or not" (an interesting point). One of them said, "Women among the people of the East are like household possessions while among the Franks, they are like spoiled children. The Franks harbor no evil thoughts about their women; even though the transgressions of these women are very numerous." He goes on to say that among their bad qualities is the lack of virtue of many of their women, as previously stated, and the lack of manly jealousy of their men (the same point again).

My last quotation comes from the Web site of the Ṭālibān in Afghanistan. This may seem improbable, but I assure you that it is so. Let me read you this:

Men in the West have made women an object of their lusts and desires; they have used them as they pleased. When these slaves of their desires had to go to work, to offices and factories, they drafted the women along with them also. Women were made to work in offices, restaurants, shops and factories for the gratification of male desires. In this way did Western man destroy the personality, position and identity of woman. The woman of the West labors under a double burden: one—she is torn by anxiety as to who will look after her in case she remains unmarried; she is thus forced to wander from door to door in search of security. Even in the matter of dress, she is exploited: men wear trousers which cover their ankles, while women are forced to wear skirts with their legs bare in every kind of weather. In the scantiest of dresses, merely a sleeveless blouse and a miniskirt, the Western woman can be seen roaming in the shops, airports, stations etc. She is a target for unscrupulous men who satisfy their lust with them wherever, whenever they please. She has become no less than a bitch, chased by a dozen dogs in heat. If these are the rights of Western women, then the West is welcome to them."

All this raises the inevitable question: Where do we go from here? It is a common belief—but an inaccurate one—that women's rights are part of a liberal, democratic program. That seems a natural, obvious assumption. In fact, it has not been so. Insofar as Middle Eastern societies respect public opinion, they cut down on women's rights, because public opinion is overwhelmingly against them. And where we do really find progress in giving political and other rights to women? It is in countries under autocratic rule: the two first notable examples were Kemal Atatürk in Turkey and the late shah in Iran. Both of these carried through programs of what I can only describe as feminist reforms. Atatürk was quite explicit about it: very soon after becoming president of the republic, he went on a tour, making speeches on women's rights, and anything less likely than an Ottoman pasha campaigning on a feminist program would be difficult to imagine. But he did just that, and he stated his reason very clearly: our task is to catch up with the modern world; we will not catch up with the modern world if we only modernize half the population. And he did what he could to achieve that result, very much against public opinion in the country at the time. Even he had limits to what he could do: he abolished traditional Islamic male headgear by law and by force; the abolition of the veil was not a legal ban but done by social pressure, and it has been coming back in various ways in Turkey at the present time. The shah was less explicit and less programmatic about it, but under the first and second shahs of the Pahlavi line, there was nevertheless a program of rights for women. Atatürk categorically abolished polygamy; monogamy was the law. In Iran, it was a little less simple than that, but it was de facto: taking a second wife was hedged around with all kinds of difficulties, which meant de facto monogamy.

Another country where there was considerable progress under authoritarian rule was Tunisia, which has one of the best records in providing education for women. Another, which may come as a surprise, is Iraq, where authoritarian rulers gave women a much more active part in public and social life than in most other Arab countries. I remember being told by Egyptian friends of mine that when they wanted to publish feminist articles, they could not do it in Egypt; they sent them to Iraq to be published there. Obviously, the Egyptian press was much freer than the Iraqi press, but the Iraqi press would publish feminist articles, and the Egyptian press, at that time, would not.

There has, of course, been a very strong reaction against this. I quoted Sayyid Qutb, who saw feminism and female emancipation as part of the ultimate wickedness of the West. We find the same in the writings of the late Ayatollah Khomeini, for whom one of the principal crimes of the monarchy was giving women rights and countermanding the Sharī'a: the shah had raised the legal age of marriage to eighteen, and the revolution brought it back to where it was before—nine: that is to say nine lunar years—it could actually be slightly less than nine solar years. That is now the legal age of marriage in the Islamic Republic; this was the age of 'Āyisha, the last of the Prophet's wives, when he married her.

Where do we go from here? The outlook is very problematic. Although there are powerful forces engaged in the repression of women and women's rights, I remain on the whole cautiously optimistic; indeed, I would go so far as to say that women, the depressed part of the population, probably represent the best hope for progress in the Islamic world.

SEVEN

Democracy and Religion in the Middle East

OR MOST OF THE TWENTIETH CENTURY, TWO IDEAS dominated political debate in the Middle East: nationalism and socialism. Sometimes the one, sometimes the other, and sometimes the two in the devastating combination of national socialism exercised enormous attraction. Both were of European origin; both from time to time enjoyed the active support of European powers. Both were adapted in various ways and with varying success to Middle Eastern conditions and needs. They gained at times passionate support and helped to accomplish significant major changes.

By the end of the century, both had lost most of their appeal. Of the two, socialism is the more seriously discredited—on the one hand, by the collapse of its superpower patron, the Soviet Union; on the other, perhaps more cogently, by the failure of Middle Eastern and North African regimes professing one or another kind of socialism to lead their people into the promised land. Instead of freedom and prosperity, they delivered tyranny and poverty, in increasingly obvious contrast with the democratic world.

Nationalism was not discredited but rather superseded by the attainment of its main objective and the consequences that followed that attainment. With the advent of full national independence, it became increasingly clear that freedom and independence were different things. In some definitions of independence, they even appeared to be incompatible.

Nationalist aims have been achieved; socialist hopes have been abandoned. But the two basic problems they were designed to remedy—deprivation and subjugation—remain and are, if anything, becoming worse. The population explosion has made the poor poorer and more numerous; the communications revolution has made them far more aware of their poverty. The departure of imperial garrisons and proconsuls has removed the most plausible excuse for the powerlessness and economic backwardness of the Muslim Middle East as contrasted, not only with the West but also with the rising powers of Asia and the near challenge of Israel. The problems remain and are becoming more serious and more visible. The search for solutions is still in progress.

When General Bonaparte invaded and occupied Egypt in 1798—an event that, by the consensus of historians, inaugurated the modern history of the Middle East—there were only two independent powers in the region, Turkey and Iran. During the era of imperialist rivalries and domination, both managed, though often with considerable difficulty, to preserve their sovereign independence. The breakup of the empires—British, French, Italian, and, most recently, Russian—made possible the emergence of a whole series of new independent states. Some of these, like Egypt and Morocco, are sustained by a sense of distinctive national identity going back centuries or even, for Egypt, millennia. But most are new constructs of uncertain and shifting identity. On the one hand, these states were long threatened by movements aiming at merging them into larger, vaguer identities, like pan-Arabism or pan-Turkism. More recently, they have been threatened from below, by regional, sectarian, ethnic, and tribal loyalties that endanger the very existence of the sovereign state. The Lebanese civil wars demonstrated where this can lead. The Lebanese paradigm could well apply in other countries like Syria and Saudi Arabia—both of them, in their present form, twentieth-century creations assembled from very diverse elements.

Turkey and Iran, in contrast, are old states, each with a deeply rooted, widely disseminated sense of common nationhood and political identity, and each with centuries of experience in the exercise of sovereign, independent government. The resulting sense of stability and continuity has enabled them to survive crises that would have shattered more fragile nations. Both also have traditions of leadership: Iran as the cultural center of a zone extending eastward into Central Asia and India, and westward into the Ottoman lands; Turkey as the leader and model of the Middle East, first in Islamic empire, then in nationalist self-liberation. And since the beginning of the sixteenth century, when the Sunni sultan of Turkey and the Shi'ite shah of Iran fought the first of a long series of wars between their two countries, they have been rivals for the leadership of the whole Middle Eastern region. In modern times, again, they have exemplified in their forms of government rival models for the future: secular democracy and religious fundamentalism.

Both terms need closer definition. The word *democracy* has been widely used in our time, in many different places with very different meanings. Often it is preceded by some modifying adjective—"popular," "guided," "basic," "organic," and the like—the effect of which is to dilute, deflect, or even reverse its meaning. There are many who claim that their cause alone— their religion, sect, party, ideology—is the only genuine democracy, and all the others are false. All these claims are, of course, true—provided that one accepts the claimant's definition of democracy. I do not, and such claims are therefore irrelevant to my present discussion. What I mean is a method of choosing, installing, and, when necessary, removing governments that evolved over centuries in the English-speaking countries and has in modern times been transplanted, with varying success, to other parts of the world. It differs from nondemocratic polities in that governments are empowered or at least confirmed by the people, normally through elections held at fixed intervals and under known and established rules that are the same for all parties. It differs from other systems that use the name of democracy in that governments can be and frequently are changed by elections, in contrast to the other, where elections are changed by governments. Democratic elections require secret polls and public counts; in pseudo democracies, the reverse is more usual. The need to face their electors at fixed intervals is usually enough to ensure that governments respect such other democratic requirements as human rights, free speech, and the rule of law.

Not all democracies are legally secular. In Britain, where representative, parliamentary democracy has the oldest roots, there is—if only in form—an established church. The same is true of some other European democracies. But elsewhere, notably in the United States and in France since the late nineteenth century, the principle was adopted of a separation between religion and the state, introduced with a double purpose: to prevent the state from interfering in religious matters and to prevent religious authorities from using the power of the state to impose and enforce their doctrines or to obtain privileges.

Religion, like *democracy*, is a word of many meanings and interpretations. Even the names of specific religions— Christianity, Islam, Judaism—convey variant and sometimes contradictory meanings to different adherents and observers. Christianity and Judaism are both very much minority religions in the Middle East as a whole. Christianity has been steadily losing ground in the central lands, both demographically and politically. It may be strengthened by the return to the region of two Christian states, Armenia and Georgia, but so far their effect has been very limited. Judaism has been virtually extinguished in most of the Arab countries; it survives among small and dwindling minorities in Morocco, Turkey, Iran, and the former Soviet republics. It is the majority—and dominant— religion of Israel.

For the vast majority of the peoples of the Middle East, religion means, and has for many centuries meant, Islam. In almost all those Arab states that have written constitutions, Islam figures either as the religion of the state or as the "principal source of legislation." The Saudis have no written constitution, arguing that the Quran or Islam itself is their constitution. The former Soviet republics have, for the most part, kept the secularist forms, though these are sometimes under challenge.

Turkey has hither to been explicitly secularist. The first legal step in this direction came in April 1928, when Article II of the constitution was amended by the deletion of the words "the religion of the Turkish State is Islam," with consequential changes in other articles removing references to religion and to holy law. A second change came in February 1937, when Article II was again amended to include the principles of the Republican People's Party, declaring the Turkish state to be "republican, nationalist, populist, étatist, secular and reformist." The principle of secularism, or more precisely of the separation of religion and the state, was maintained through several subsequent constitutional changes. It is in this sense that the English word *secularism* in used here, as the equivalent of the French *laïcité*, the German *laizität*, and adaptations in other languages. Unfortunately, this word is not used in English, and misunderstanding occasionally arises from the irreligious and antireligious connotations sometimes attached to the words *secularism* and *secularist*. The same ambiguity caused some problems in Turkish when the issue was first raised, and *secular* was rendered by the term *lā-dīnī*, which could be understood both as nonreligious and as irreligious.

It was later replaced by *lâik*, from the French *laique*. Turkish "laicism" has faced and is facing several challenges, most recently from the twice elected government in power.

The crucial distinction in Middle Eastern Islam at the present time is between those movements to which we of the West have attached the name "Islamic fundamentalism" and the rest, which, for want of a better term, we might, for the time being at least, call "mainstream Islam." The name *fundamentalism* is, for various reasons, inappropriate and even misleading. It came into use in the United States to designate certain Protestant churches that differed from mainstream Protestantism. There were two main points of difference, liberal theology and biblical criticism, both of which they rejected. A basic fundamentalist doctrine was the literal divinity and inerrancy of the biblical text.

These are not the concerns of the so-called Islamic fundamentalists. Liberal theology of a kind has been an issue among Muslims in the past; it may again be an issue among Muslims in the future. But it is not an important issue at the present time, and it is not about theology that fundamentalists and mainstream Muslims differ. Nor is scripture criticism an issue. All Muslims, believing, practicing, or merely conforming, accept the divinity and inerrancy of the Quranic text, or at least do not question it in public. This, again, is not the issue that divides fundamentalists from mainstream Muslims.

The term *fundamentalist* is thus rightly condemned, as inappropriate since it is American and Protestant and therefore irrelevant to Islam, and is inaccurate since it refers to doctrinal issues quite different from those that concern Muslims. Some have also criticized it as derogatory—a term that prejudges and condemns the movements, ideas, and individuals it purports to denote.

Unfortunately, the substitutes that have been proposed and are sometimes used are as bad or even worse. The most frequent, *Islamist* and *Islamism*, could be misleading, since they imply that these movements are a characteristic expression of Muslim beliefs and behavior. Precisely for this reason, the fundamentalists themselves welcome and use this term, while other Muslims hesitate. Of late, literal translations of the English word *fundamentalist* have come into use in Arabic, Persian, Turkish, and no doubt, other languages used by Muslims. By now, *fundamentalism* is more often used of Muslims than of American Protestants, and the danger of misunderstanding applies more to the latter than to the former. A word which has been adopted in the languages of Islam to designate a Muslim group may surely be retained in the languages of Christendom.

In discussing the attitudes and activities of Muslim fundamentalists, two facts—self-evident when stated, but often forgotten—must be recognized: first, that most Muslims are not fundamentalists, and second, that most fundamentalists are not terrorists. Fundamentalists, naturally, are concerned to obscure or revise the first of these facts; terrorists find it expedient to obscure the second. Both are helped in achieving these aims, on the one hand by the media, which naturally and perhaps inevitably give far more attention to the violent minority than to the law-abiding majority, and on the other by some Muslim leaders, both religious and political, who feel unwilling or unable to condemn terrorist groups and acts in unequivocal terms. Of late, there has been an alarming increase in manifestations of popular support for terrorist actions and slogans, all over the Muslim world and especially in the Muslim diaspora in Europe and the Americas.

Islamic fundamentalism remains a powerful and, in some areas, a growing force. Fundamentalist groups differ from country to country or even, on occasion, within a single country, sometimes cooperating, sometimes competing for support. They are usually ready to cooperate against the infidel enemy, postponing their own feuds until after victory. Thus, even the radical Shī'a leadership of Iran and the radical anti-Shī'a Wahhābis of al Qaeda have, it would seem, been able on occasion to work together in the greater jihad.

There have, in the centuries of Islamic history, been many such movements—radical, subversive, often violent, seeking the overthrow of the existing order and its replacement by one more authentically Islamic. Sometimes these movements have been directed against a foreign target. Much more frequently, their activities have been directed against their own Muslim—or, as they would say, nominally Muslim—leaders and regimes, whom they accuse of abandoning authentic Islam and adopting foreign and infidel ways. One of the major grievances against foreign powers is their support for such regimes, increasingly seen as their puppets. The fundamentalists' aim is to end this corruption of Islamic society and restore the God-given holy law of Islam. Such rulers and regimes are, in their view, worse than infidels; they are apostates, and the penalty for apostasy is death. The shah of Iran and President Sadat of Egypt were seen as such apostates. In Egypt, fundamentalists killed the ruler; in Iran, they were more successful and overthrew the regime.

In both countries, as also in Algeria, in the Sudan, and elsewhere, the Islamic fundamentalist attack was not initially directed against the West. It was directed against what for them was a far greater danger—against Muslims who slavishly imitate the West and allow Western depravity to corrode and destroy Islamic society.

Yet in opposing Westernization, the fundamentalists adopt much that is Western: Western technology and especially weaponry, Western communications, and even, in Iran, such Western inventions as a written constitution and an elected parliament. The Islamic Republic of Iran has both, though neither has any precedent in Islamic history or doctrine. Iran even has contested elections with rival candidates who conduct competing campaigns. There are, however, strict limits. In Turkish general elections in recent years, increasing numbers of the electorate have voted for an Islamic party, to the point where it was able to win parliamentary majorities and form the government of the republic. Their present declared position is that they are Muslim democrats the way that some parties in continental Europe are Christian democrats, without challenging the secular basis of the constitution. Some of their critics see them as a serious threat to the achievements of the Kemalist revolution. We do not know how many Iranians would vote for a secular democratic party, since that option is not allowed to them, but there are growing indications that many if not most Iranians would welcome such a change. It is now possible to imagine a future situation in which Turkey and Iran exchange roles as the rival champions of Islamic theocracy and secular democracy.

At this stage, it may be useful to attempt a typology of the existing regimes in the Islamic countries of the Middle East and North Africa. They may be classified as follows:

1. Traditional Autocracies. There was a time when virtually all the regimes of the Islamic world would have qualified for this description. Those that remain at the present time are principally the dynastic regimes of Saudi Arabia and of the Arabian shore of the Gulf and the Indian Ocean. These regimes are monarchical and authoritarian and, for the most part, dispense with such frills as constitutions and elected assemblies. Their origins are tribal, and tribal leadership depends on the freely given and always revocable acceptance of the tribesmen. This, though hardly democratic, is in origin at least consensual. The tribal and Islamic traditions that sustain them also limit them. Islamic law and custom, while allowing autocratic power to the ruler, nevertheless maintain that even the ruler himself is subject to the law and not above it. These constraints are no longer as effective as they were, since modern technology and weaponry have at once strengthened the sovereign power and weakened the intermediate powers that once limited it. But the same modern technology is also available to—and is increasingly being used by—those who seek to overthrow the existing authority.

2. Liberalizing Autocracies. These regimes—Morocco, some of the Gulf states, Jordan, and for a while Egypt—are rooted in traditional autocracy but take significant steps toward modernization and therefore, inevitably, toward democratization. They are no longer traditional autocracies; they are not yet liberal democracies, but the overall movement is toward greater freedom. In some, development is still hampered by failed public enterprises—a residue of the socialist era. Others are making some progress in economic, social, and human development.

3. Dictatorships. This term is often used loosely and inaccurately to designate regimes that would more appropriately be described as authoritarian or autocratic. It may be used with greater precision of the one-party regimes maintained by Hafiz al-Asad and his son in Syria and, until recently, by Saddam Hussein in Iraq, both clearly modeled on the European one-party regimes of the 1930s and 1940s. Both countries were administered directly under mandate in the interwar period— Syria by France, Iraq by Britain. Both mandatary powers created democratic institutions in their own image—a constitutional and parliamentary monarchy in Iraq, a parliamentary republic in Syria. Neither struck deep roots, and both were dismantled not long after the departure of the mandatary powers. In Syria and Iraq, as in Germany and Italy, the one-party dictatorships were erected on the ruins of unsuccessful democratic experiments. Here, the connection was direct. After the French surrender in 1940, the French authorities in Syria-Lebanon chose to rally to Vichy rather than to DeGaulle. Syria-Lebanon now became a major base for Nazi propaganda and activity in the Arab world. For a while, the Nazis and their Arab collaborators were remarkably successful and even extended their activities to Iraq, where they established, under Rashīd ʿAlī, a pro-Axis fascist-style government. It was in this period that we may find the antecedents of the Baʿth parties of both Syria and Lebanon—a fairly close imitation of the Nazi or Fascist use of the term *party*. The

Allied victories in the Middle East for a while ended this phase, but the Allied withdrawal after the war, followed by the arrival and establishment of the Soviets, brought a revival of the Ba'th Party, this time under different auspices. The adaptation from the Nazi model to the Communist model presented no great difficulty. This was the only European importation that really worked in the Middle East, and it is there, rather than in the Arab or Islamic past, that one must seek the roots of Saddam Hussein's distinctive type of government.

4. The Ex-Soviet Republics. This group, classified by history and geography rather than by regime type, consists of the six former Soviet republics with mostly Muslim populations in Transcaucasia and Central Asia. Like the former British and French dependencies in southwest Asia and North Africa in the interwar period, they had some difficulty in disentangling themselves from their former imperial masters. After the formal recognition of independence came the post–imperial hangover— a period of interference, of unequal treaties, and of "bases" and "advisers" and the like. The formative influences that have shaped their history for the last century or more are very different from those of the former British and French imperial territories. Their problems have also been different in that they were dealing not with London or Paris but with Moscow.

5. Revolutionary Islamic Regimes. The term *revolution* has been frequently used in the modern Middle East to designate a series of palace and military seizures of power that might more accurately be denoted by such terms as the French *coup d'état*, the German *putsch*, or the Spanish *pronunciamiento*. In Iran, in 1979, power was transferred not just from one clique of individuals to another, but from one whole social order to another, with a comprehensive redistribution of political and economic authority and privilege. And as with other major revolutions, this itself was part of a longer, broader, deeper process than the immediate transfer of power. For better or for worse—the Iranians are still

sharply divided on this—what happened in Iran was a major revolution in the full sense of the word. Like eighteenth-century France and twentieth–century Russia, Iran has gone through the classical stages: upheaval and repression, terror and revolutionary justice, intervention and war, ideological debate and political conflict, and vast social transformations. The price of revolution is familiar and has been paid at a high rate. The returns are, as so often, problematic. Like the French and Russian revolutions, the Iranian revolution evoked a powerful response in other Muslim countries with which the Iranians shared a common universe of discourse. Like the Jacobins and the Bolsheviks in their day, the Iran-based Islamic radicals of our time have encouraged—and sometimes organized and directed—a whole series of movements in these countries. The Iranian revolution now appears to have reached what might variously be described as its Napoleonic or Stalinist phase.

6. Democracies in the Western sense of the word—that is, political systems in which free elections are held and governments may be removed by the decision of the electorate. Many countries in the region hold elections—partly because this is the fashionable attire of the modern state, partly because some form of election is sometimes necessary to qualify for international respect and on occasion aid. But in most of these regimes, elections are a ceremonial ratification of the realities of power. There are only two states in the region where genuine elections are held and governments can be—and sometimes are—changed by elections: Turkey and Israel.

A crucial question arises and is often asked in all these countries: Is Islam compatible with democracy? The same question has been asked in broader terms: Is religion compatible with democracy? In the sense of a system of belief and worship, of morality and conduct, the answer is clearly yes. But if we use "religion" in the sense of a complex of historical experiences and cultural traditions, the answer may vary. One could, for example, purely on the basis of the historical record, give different answers for Orthodox, Catholic, and Protestant Christianity. For Judaism, there can as yet be no answer, since ancient memories are too remote and recent experience too brief to provide any basis for one. For Islam, there is the record of more than fourteen centuries of history and, at the present time, the political life of more than fifty Muslim sovereign states.

At first sight, neither the one nor the other offers much ground for optimism. Islamic history is a record of unrelieved autocracy: rarely despotic, often benign and enlightened, usually limited by the provisions of the holy law, but with no tradition of corporate bodies, of representation, or of majority decision. The first four caliphs who ruled after the death of the Prophet Muhammad are known among Sunni Muslims as "the rightly guided caliphs," and the period of their rule is regarded as the golden age of Islam. Of the four, three were assassinated—one by a disgruntled slave, the other two by rebellious Muslims—and their rule foundered in the first of a series of civil wars. Of the present Muslim states in the Middle East, only one, the Turkish Republic, can be called a democracy in any serious sense. There are a few other states that seem to be moving in this direction, but none has moved as far as Turkey—and even Turkish democracy has endured reverses and interruptions.

But it would be rash to conclude that because democracy has not worked in the past, it will not work in the future. The countries in the rest of the world where stable democratic institutions have functioned smoothly over long periods are very few indeed. In most others, the recent spread of democratic institutions must still be regarded as experimental. The record of democracy even in most of continental Europe is, at best, checkered, and it would be unreasonable to expect better and faster results in regions of very different culture. After all, even American democracy was, for a while, deemed compatible with the maintenance of slavery and for a much longer period with the complete disenfranchisement of half the population—the female half. In the first democratic experiments in the Middle East, members of religious minorities were the strongest supporters, since they hoped that a democratic order would give them the equality which the old order had denied them. Women may well cherish the same hope. They are far more numerous than the Christian and Jewish minorities, and unlike these minorities, they are indispensable. Women may yet be the greatest upholders of democracy in the Islamic lands. They are certainly the group with the most to lose by its failure.

But the Middle East is predominantly Muslim and dominantly male, and the institutions that Middle Eastern Muslims create and operate will inevitably be shaped to a significant degree by their cultural and historical traditions and memories.

While these have in the past presented some barriers to the development of democratic institutions, they also contain positive elements that, rightly interpreted and applied, might lead to greater political freedom and respect for human rights. There have been many attempts by supporters of democracy to find elements in the Muslim religious heritage that could point in the direction of democratic freedom. Some of these arguments have been of variable cogency and limited effect. But there are elements—not strained interpretations of marginal texts, but central to Islamic history and tradition—that could indeed be conducive to the development of democratic institutions.

The formative scriptural narratives of Islam are very different from those of Judaism and Christianity. Moses was not permitted to enter the Promised Land, and the Hebrew Bible is dominated by the themes of bondage and liberation, exile and return. Christ was crucified, and his followers suffered and endured for centuries as a persecuted minority before finally capturing the state and—some would add—being captured by it. Muhammad conquered his promised land and founded his own state. The Qur'ān records his struggles, his victories, and his achievements as ruler—promulgating laws, dispensing justice, making war, making peace. The separation of church and state—a Christian solution to a Christian dilemma—had little or no meaning in the classical Islamic context.

Islamic teachings and Islamic law do, however, recognize a difference between the things of this world and the things of the next. That recognition is embodied in the extensive literature devoted by Muslim jurists and theologians to the problems of state and sovereignty. From the earliest times, this was a matter of great concern, and Muslims, philosophers, jurists and others reflected carefully on the nature of political power; on the ways in which it might be acquired and used and, if need be, forfeited; and on the duties and responsibilities, as well as the rights and privileges, of those who hold it. The discussion and regulation of these matters form a central part of the Sharī'a the holy law of Islam.

A study of the rich political literature produced by Islamic scholarship reveals a conception of sovereignty that is very remote from the arbitrary despotism often ascribed to Islam by outsiders. The headship of the community—the caliphate—as defined by Sunni jurists is both contractual and consensual. A new caliph is installed by a *bay'a* between the ruler and the ruled. This word is often translated as "homage." It might be better translated as "contract" or even "deal." The *bay'a* creates bonds of obligation between the ruler and the subjects. The latter are duty-bound to obey the ruler, but the ruler also has duties toward the subjects. Much of what in Western political thought is discussed under the heading of "the rights of the citizen" appears in Muslim writings under the heading of "the duties of the ruler." If the ruler defaults on his obligations or becomes incapable of fulfilling them, the contract can, in principle, be dissolved. Though historically this is very rare, there are precedents.

The duty of obedience is extensive and comprehensive, but it is not unlimited. Two dicta attributed to the Prophet himself

are cited on this point. One of them says: "Do not obey a creature against his Creator"; that is, do not obey a human command
to violate divine law. The same point is made in another saying:
"There is no obedience in sin." What this implies is not just a
right of disobedience, as in much Western thought, but a divinely
ordained duty of disobedience against the sinful orders of a
sinful ruler. This principle was invoked both by those who
murdered Sadat and those who overthrew the shah. As a check
on autocracy, this rule was of limited effect. The holy law itself
assigns almost absolute powers to the caliph and provides no
testing device to determine whether an order—or, for that
matter, a ruler—is sinful. But rebellions and depositions are not
unknown in Muslim history, and the principle is still there to be
invoked.

According to another saying traditionally ascribed to the
Prophet: "Difference of opinion within my community is God's
mercy." In other words, diversity is good, something to be
welcomed, not suppressed. On this point, the realities of Muslim
history are closer to the principles of Muslim doctrine than in
the matter of contractual and consensual sovereignty. In modern
times, there has been a sad falling away from the easygoing tolerance of earlier days, but here again, the principle is there to be
invoked.

One other point that may be added is the emphasis in Islamic
tradition on the twin qualities of dignity and humility. Even the
humblest of subjects are accorded personal dignity in the traditional social order, and rulers were expected to avoid arrogance.
According to old Ottoman custom, when the sultan received the
state dignitaries on religious holidays, he rose to his feet to greet
the Chief Qadis, as a sign of his respect for the law. When a new
sultan was installed, he was greeted by the people with cries of
"Sultan, be not proud! God is greater than you!"

Freedom as a political ideal was new and alien. The words *free*
and *freedom* in classical Islamic usage had a legal and social

meaning, not a political meaning. The primary meaning of free is the converse of slave. It is also occasionally used in a social sense to connote some fiscal and other exemptions, and occasionally in a moral sense to note nobility (cf. French *franchise*) of character and behavior. Its political meaning was learned from Europe, and the lesson was driven home by the imperial powers.

These—principally Britain, France, Holland, and Russia—deprived most of the Islamic world of sovereignty. The prime demand, therefore, was for independence. Foreign rule was seen as tyranny, and the overriding political aim was to end it. But tyranny means different things in different cultures. In Western political thought, the converse of tyranny is freedom. In the traditional Islamic system, the converse of tyranny is justice. At the present time, most Muslim countries are discovering that while they have gained independence, they enjoy neither justice or freedom. There are some in the region—and their number is increasing—who see in democracy a way to attain both.

EIGHT

Peace and Freedom in the Middle East

It is often said and generally agreed that democracies do not make war. Democratic governments are elected by the people and are answerable to the people, and with exceedingly rare exceptions, the people prefer peace. It is equally true, though less recognized, that dictatorships do not make peace. The world war started by the Third Reich ended with its defeat. The Cold War started by the Soviet Union ended with its collapse.

In the same way, the dictatorships that rule much of the Middle East today will not—indeed, cannot—make peace because they need conflict to justify their tyrannical oppression of their own people and to deflect their people's anger against an external enemy. As with the Third Reich and the Soviet Union, real peace will come only with their defeat or, preferably, collapse and their replacement by governments that have been chosen and can be dismissed by their people and will therefore seek to resolve, not provoke, conflicts.

For some time past, it has been our custom in the West to identify ourselves as "the Free World" because of the democratic institutions we see as an essential part of what defines our common identity. It also serves to demarcate the contrast between ourselves and the unfree world. Until recently, this meant, first and foremost, the Soviet Union and its dependencies, living under Communist tyranny. It also served to-differentiate us from the so-called Third World, most of which was governed by a variety of indigenous autocracies, and the rest enjoyed partially or dubiously free institutions of a kind. Some would argue that such free institutions as exist were installed and bequeathed by former imperial rulers; others, that it is the lingering remnants of colonial rule and post–colonial influence that have prevented the achievement of true freedom. Both claims are, to say the least, plausible.

In all the languages of the Middle East—in Arabic, Persian, Turkish, and Hebrew alike—the words used for "free" and "freedom" are in origin legal terms, denoting the status of the free man or woman as opposed to the slave. Occasionally, the word *free* denoted membership of a privileged class and conveyed the meaning of "exempt," usually in a fiscal and administrative sense. The traditional Islamic ideal of good government, the converse of tyranny, is defined as justice, not freedom. The political meaning of free and freedom derives from European usage and ultimately from Rome and Greece. The earliest Middle Eastern reference known to me occurs during the Jewish revolt against Roman power, led by Bar-Kokhba in 132 to 135 C.E. Although ultimately crushed, Bar-Kokhba was able to seize and briefly hold Jerusalem, and to celebrate this victory, he struck a coin with the inscription *Herut Yerushalayim*, the "freedom of Jerusalem." The use of this term with a political rather than a legal or social meaning, and in relation to a city and not a person, is a departure from previous usage and clearly reflects the influence of Greek thought and practice. In modern times, the impact of the West produced a similar semantic evolution in the cognate Arabic term *ḥurriyya*, "freedom."

In the Middle East in modern times, freedom has become a central theme of political aspiration. Until the ending of colonial rule, it was commonly used to express an objective more accurately designated by the term *independence*. But the attainment of nationalist objectives did not bring freedom, only the replacement of foreign overlords by homegrown tyrants, less constrained and more adept in their tyranny. In most countries, independence brought the loss of even the small measure of freedom allowed by imperial masters, and the word has begun to change its meaning again.

If the Turkish Republic embodied the aspiration for a modernizing secular democracy, the Islamic Republic of Iran expresses the alternative solution—the rejection of the pervasive impact of Western power and the corrupting influence of Western culture, and the aspiration to an authentic and comprehensive Islamic order. In Turkish elections, the Islamist program has been able to win majorities and form governments. In Iranian elections, the choice for secular democracy is not permitted.

Only two countries in the region can be described as working democracies in any real sense: Turkey and Israel. Both of these, in different ways and to different observers, serve as both a warning and an encouragement.

In the rest of the region, a variety of unfree and semifree regimes prevail. Egypt, with a quasi-socialist economy and a quasi-parliamentary life presidency, faces mounting pressure from advocates of both solutions, threatening both the domestic order and the foreign policy of the country.

Saudi Arabia is at once a tribal monarchy and a rigorous Islamic state, inspired by Wahhabism, the most extreme and fanatical form of Islamic fundamentalism at the present day. With the prestige of the custodianship of the holy cities and the wealth brought by oil, Saudi Arabia plays a disproportionate role in the shaping and direction of Muslim thought and action.

From the beginning, the impact of European influence and the resulting modernization brought damage as well as benefits to Middle Eastern societies. The modern instruments of surveillance and repression gave the ruler greater power than had ever been exercised before, even by the legendary tyrants of the past. At the same time, social and legal change removed or enfeebled the socioeconomic groups and traditional constraints that had previously limited the autocratic power of the ruler and the state. The result was a steady intensification of autocracy and the emergence of a new class who relied on the state, and on the use of the state apparatus, to achieve wealth and power for themselves and their families. Already at the time of the Crimean War, the point was well made by a British naval officer, Adolphus Slade, who remarked: "The old nobility lived on their estates. The State is the estate of the new nobility."

Two countries, Iraq and Syria, went all the way in adopting and applying the continental European model of the totalitarian dictatorship. The inspiration might be fascist, Nazi, or Communist, according to changing political circumstances, but in their essential methods, they did not differ greatly. Iraq until the overthrow of Saddam Hussein and Syria until today are ruled by dictators, maintaining power by a monstrous apparatus of indoctrination and repression, the one through a single party that is part of the very structure of government, and the other through the usual, ramified agencies of detection and enforcement.

Other countries in the region offer a number of variations on these patterns—some milder, some more rigorous; some secular, some religious; none of them willing to allow the unfettered discussion of their rule and policies or submit themselves to the free choice of their people.

Not surprisingly, the movement for freedom has been strongest where the oppression is severest, notably in Iran, suffering from a clerical fascist dictatorship, and Iraq, ruled by the Middle

Eastern exemplar of European totalitarianism. Democratic ideas have deep roots in these countries, and given the chance, they may soon prevail, and in so doing, inspire others. Then, and only then, will there be governments in the region that need peace, not war, to retain the allegiance of their subjects.

NINE

Democracy, Legitimacy, and Succession in the Middle East

HERE IS AN ILLUSION, CURIOUSLY WIDESPREAD IN the world at the present time, that democracy is the natural state of mankind and that any departure from democracy is either a crime to be punished or an illness to be cured. It was because of this delusion that in so many parts of the world, particularly in the last fifty years or so, the terms *democracy* and *democratic* have been, shall we say, modified and adapted to fit a whole range of different regimes. If we look at the political usage of the twentieth century, we find that often the noun *democracy* is preceded by some other term, the purpose of which is to modify, distort, or even reverse the meaning of the substantive. So we find organic democracy, people's democracy, and many others. Fortunately, few of those have survived. But the term *democracy* was used by Franco in Spain, the colonels in Greece, the generals in Pakistan, the commissars in Soviet Europe, and a whole series of regimes in different parts of Africa. When a country introduces the word *democratic* in its official title, that is a danger signal.

What do we mean by democracy? Nowadays, the term has become rather more restricted in use, and I suppose that the best definition I can offer you is one that draws neither on political science nor on history; a definition offered by Sam Huntingdon, famous for his *Clash of Civilizations*. Without committing myself on that topic, I do like his definition of *democracy*. He says you can call a country a democracy when it has changed its government twice by elections. That's a very good working definition. It has happened a number of times that a government, either on principle or through inadvertence, has allowed itself to be voted out of office, but those who came in its place have usually taken very good care not to repeat the error of their predecessors. The "twice" is important—after the second change, we can really say that the country is a working democracy.

What we are usually talking about when we use the word *democracy* is the system of government devised by the English-speaking peoples, first in England, then in countries beyond the seas where they speak English and adopt or adapt English political institutions. These distinctive forms of democracy have been experimented with in other parts. But let's be honest about it. If we look even at Europe, which prides itself in being in the forefront of democratic development, the record is, to say the least, checkered. If we take as a test of democracy, that democratic institutions have worked smoothly and without interruption for the last hundred years, that they are functioning smoothly now and that there is every likelihood that they will continue to function smoothly in the future, and then let us ask—of how many countries in continental Europe can we say that? The list would be very short.

There are now many democracies in Europe and elsewhere; they have different names, they are developing along different ways, and few of them as yet have been really tested in adversity. But democracy by Huntington's definition has had some impact in the world and is more popular than at any previous time; for example, almost the whole of South America has formally or informally adopted that type of democracy.

In most of the Middle East, the situation is somewhat different. Two countries, Turkey and Israel, do change their governments by elections, in Turkey also by other methods though not recently, but by elections many times. Apart from those two countries, the normal Middle Eastern practice is not that elections change governments but that governments change elections. A Middle Eastern election has more in common with an American inauguration or a British coronation than with an American or British election. In other words, it is a ceremonial, ritual ratification of a choice that has already been made by other methods.

What are then the essential features of democratic regimes, in contrast with others? It seems to me that there are three that are particularly relevant to a discussion of political systems in the Middle East. The first is limitation. Government is limited; whoever rules, the monarch, the president, the prime minister— his rule is limited, and it is subject to certain laws. He does not possess absolute despotic power. The second is accountability; the government, being limited, is accountable for what it does and may be called to account where it goes beyond the line, where it exceeds the authority granted to it, or where it violates the basic laws under which it operates. The third is representation, the idea that at some stage and in some form, those who participate in and conduct government should be the chosen representatives of the mass of the population.

All three of these are typical of the Western type of democracy. Limitation is ensured by a constitution, written or unwritten; accountability is ensured by some kind of legal procedure for testing the constitutionality of acts of government; and representation is ensured through some form of election. These have evolved over a very long period of time; representation, in particular, in the full sense is very modern. Until not so long ago, it was considered to be perfectly compatible with democracy to exclude slightly more than half the population from any form of participation—I refer, of course, to the female half. In some countries, democracy was considered compatible with preserving the ancient institution of slavery. But slavery has gone, and the acquisition of political rights by women has now been generally accepted in the Western world and even parts of the non-Western world, and we may now agree that representation has reached its full form in the West.

I spoke of the illusion that democracy is the natural human condition. There is a second illusion to which I would like to draw attention: the illusion that all nondemocratic forms of government, all forms of government other than Western-style democracy, all are the same, and all are bad.

This is quite untrue, on both points. There is a tremendous variety between the different forms of government that have flourished in the past and that exist at the present time, in different parts of the Middle East and in many other places in the world. They are by no means all of them bad or harmful, though that thesis is becoming increasingly difficult to maintain at the present time. In 1826, an Egyptian scholar, sheikh, from Al-Azhar Rifā'a Rāfi' al-Ṭahṭāwī went to Paris with the first Egyptian student mission to the West. He was not a member of the mission. He was sent as a religious preceptor—a chaplain, so to speak—to look after the spiritual welfare of this first batch of Muslim Egyptian students who were turned loose amid the dangers of Paris. He stayed in Paris from 1826 to 1831 and wrote an account of his travels, adventures, and observations. He seems to have learned much more than any of the pupils for whom he was responsible, and this book is a landmark in the development of political ideas in the Middle Eastern region. It was published in Arabic; it was also translated into Turkish and was for some time the only firsthand account of the contemporary West available to the Muslim reader in his own language.

In this book he makes a very profound observation. He talks about freedom—the Arabic word he uses is *ḥurriyya*. Now the word *freedom* in Arabic, until that time, was a legal term, not a political term. Freedom was the converse of slavery. If one was not a slave—that is to say, legally enslaved—then one was free. That, of course, was the meaning of freedom in Western languages originally. But whereas the West used freedom and slavery as a metaphor for good and bad government, the Islamic peoples didn't make use of that particular metaphor. Sheikh Rifā'a discusses freedom, and then he says, and this was a profound observation at the time: "when the French talk about freedom, what they mean is the same as what we mean when we talk about justice—*'adl*."

There is a vast literature on politics in classical Arabic and other languages of Islam. The state was a subject to which they devoted considerable attention and thought. Part of it is what we might call the constitutional provisions of the holy law, that part of the holy law, the Sharī'a, that deals with the formation, conduct, transfer, and termination of government. Some of the writings are philosophical; some are practical, handbooks of statecraft and the like. All this amounts to a very considerable, ramified, and sophisticated political literature in Islamic languages before the impact of Western ideas. In that literature, the antithesis between good and bad government is defined as between tyranny and justice, *ẓulm* and *'adl*.

Ẓulm combines two different notions—the notion of the tyrant and the notion of the usurper. The usurper is one who governs without being entitled to, in other words, who has no legitimacy; the tyrant is one who governs in violation of the law. What law? We'll come back to that. Thus *ẓulm* is a combination of tyranny and usurpation, with a connotation of unjust, tyrannical, illegitimate government. *'Adl* is the converse: government in accordance with the law of God by a ruler who is entitled to be the ruler and who governs in accordance with those rules.

Sheikh Rifā'a was making a rather astute observation when he equated the Muslim notion of *'adl* with the European notion of freedom.

Let us look a little closer at this Muslim notion of *'adl*, as defined by the Sharī'a. There is in almost every legal treatise a chapter, usually the first chapter, dealing with the headship of the state. According to the rules as set forth, the headship of the state, the office of the caliph, has three remarkable features: it is contractual, it is consensual, and it is limited. It is contractual in the sense that there is an agreement. The new caliph becomes caliph—I'm speaking of the law, not what actually happened—because there is an agreement between him and a suitable body of the believers. The law is vague on what constitutes a suitable body—how large, how many, who, and so on. They found it perhaps expedient to leave that unspecified. But nevertheless the notion of contract is there. And when they agree, there is what is called a *bay'a*.

Bay'a is usually translated as homage or allegiance; a more accurate translation would be a deal; it is an agreement between the new ruler and his new subjects, that he will command and they will obey, subject to certain rules and regulations. That is clearly a contractual element, in theory at least, according to the holy law.

It is also consensual in that it is in principle voluntary, not imposed. He becomes caliph with the consent of those with whom the *bay'a* is contracted. The law books frequently quote two hadiths, sayings attributed to the Prophet. One says, "there is no obedience in sin." The other says, "do not obey a creature against the Creator." The meaning of these traditions is clear. If the imam or if the caliph issues a commandment that is contrary to Sharī'a, then the duty of obedience, which otherwise prevails, lapses, and what arises in its place is not merely a right of disobedience, such as we find in Western political thought, but a duty of disobedience. This gives rise to interesting possibilities in theory and more especially in practice. The third point is that it is limited. He holds his office under Shari'a; he is supposed to conduct himself according to Shari'a.

That is the theory that is frequently invoked. How did it work out? What, for example, did accountability mean? To whom is the ruler accountable? In Western democratic systems, he is accountable to the people. In the Islamic Middle East, this was an alien notion. There, he is accountable to God, and there are many traditions, the general purport of which is that if the ruler is cruel and tyrannical, he will be punished and the subjects will be rewarded, presumably in the afterlife. Accountability is to God; God will make the necessary arrangements and will reward the long-suffering but obedient subjects and punish the evil-doing ruler.

Some were not entirely satisfied with that and devised what we might call a theory of revolution. The question of accountability could also take another aspect. If the ruler is accountable to God, who represents God? In the Islamic world, in contrast with Christendom, there was no such thing as an ecclesiastical institution. The great Christian debate between church and state had no equivalent in Islamic history until comparatively modern times. Church and state were one and the same. The founder of Islam, the Prophet Muhammad, unlike his predecessors Moses and Jesus, became the head of the state. He was a ruler and an administrator. He not only promulgated the law but also applied and enforced it. So there was no ecclesiastical institution, and generally speaking, the men of the holy law were more or less submissive to the state. It was even regarded as demeaning to have anything to do with the state. If we look, for example, at pious biographies—we have literally hundreds of thousands of traditional biographies of pious ulema—one of the tropes that comes again and again as measure of piety is that he was asked to accept an appointment under the state and refused. The offer demonstrates his learning; the refusal, his piety.

It wasn't until comparatively modern times—no doubt inspired by the example of Christian institutions, though, of course, they would not admit that—that they began to develop an ecclesiastical institution. This has reached its apex in the modern Republic of Iran, where we find the institutional, though not the doctrinal, equivalents of a pope, a college of cardinals, a bench of bishops, and an inquisition, none of which had any previous existence in Islamic history. And having Christianized their institutions to that extent, I have no doubt that sooner rather than later they will have the next step, a reformation. But that takes us away from our immediate topic.

Accountability is therefore present in principle but often of limited value in actually checking the misdeeds of a tyrannical ruler. On the whole, though, the legal rules were remarkably effective, and rulers were obedient to the main provisions of the Shari'a. We do not find open and public violations of major Shari'a principles, and rulers usually managed to stay within the rather broadly defined limits imposed by the holy law. The outrageous tyrants that we find, for example, in later Roman times or in present-day Middle Eastern countries have no equivalent in classical Islamic states from the early caliphate down to the Ottomans.

What is entirely lacking in the Middle Eastern political tradition is representation and what goes with it—the idea that people elect others to represent them, that these others meet in some sort of corporate body, and that that corporate body deliberates, conducts discussions, and, most important of all, reaches decisions that have binding force. Corporate bodies, corporate decision—these are unknown to the classical political traditions of the region. We do not even find corporate bodies in the more purely legal sense. In Roman law and in most of the European systems derived from it or influenced by it, there is such a thing as a legal person, a corporation, an abstraction that nevertheless functions as a legal person. There is no equivalent in Islamic law, with the partial exception of the *waqf*, but that has not had any political significance. There was no such thing as the city, for example. There was a conglomeration of quarters, neighborhoods, houses, families, but no city as a legally, politically constituted entity, and we have interesting documents on the introduction of municipal institutions as part of the Ottoman reforms in the mid-nineteenth century. This was a brand-new idea and involved new problems of adaptation and adjustment. And since there were no corporate bodies of that kind, there were, of course, no equivalents of the corporate institutions that existed in ancient Greece and Rome, of the Sanhedrin among the ancient Jews, and of all the various derivatives in Christian Europe and its area of cultural expansion beyond the seas.

The effect of modernization at first seemed to be in the direction of greater democracy. Middle Eastern rulers in Egypt, in Turkey, and later in Iran created parliaments. They held elections, they created legislative bodies, and they devolved authority to municipalities, to councils, and so on, so that at first sight one might say that the nineteenth-century reforms brought a greater degree of democracy, or at any rate, a move toward democratization. Unfortunately, exactly the opposite happened. The new machinery, the new apparatus of government, communication, warfare, and the rest that the nineteenth century brought had two major effects.

One was the abrogation of intermediate powers. In the past, the authority of the sovereign, though in theory almost absolute, subject only to Shari'a, was in fact limited by all kinds of established and entrenched powers—the country gentry, provincial notables, the urban patricians, the guilds, and the well-established military units like the Corps of Janissaries continuing from generation to generation. A British naval officer, Adolphus Slade, looking at Turkey in the 1830s, observed that they also had a kind of revolutionary democracy and suggested the sometimes mutinous Corps of Janissaries as the equivalent of the Chamber of Deputies in Paris. This is not altogether an absurd comparison. These bodies did have a function in limiting the absolute power of the sovereign. The effect of modernization was to abrogate or enfeeble these limiting powers, one by one. The ulema, who had previously been one of the most important of the limiting powers, were, so to speak, nationalized. They had previously been a separate institution; they were now taken over by the state and became salaried civil servants.

The modernization of the armed forces—of weaponry, travel, and communication—had also a second effect. While abrogating intermediate powers, they greatly strengthened the sovereign power, so that a late-nineteenth-century ruler like the Ottoman sultan Abdulhamid II was able to exercise a degree of authority that none of the great sultans of the past had had. He could communicate by telegraph with his provincial governors, and he could send heavily armed troops by train. Suleyman the Magnificent could not do either of these. So the effect of modernization in most of these countries in the nineteenth and early twentieth centuries was to create a level of absolutism far greater than had ever existed in the fabled past. This continued with such modern regimes as those of Saddam Hussein in Iraq and the late Hafiz al-Asad in Syria. One could add other, perhaps less obvious, examples.

But there is one glimmer of hope in this, that the current form of modernization, particularly the modernization of communications, has now begun to reverse that trend. The first electronic revolution in history, as far as I am aware, is that which brought about the overthrow of the shah and the enthronement—I use the word advisedly—of the Ayatollah Khomeini. This was a revolution conducted by telephone and cassette. Since then, the means available have been vastly improved. A revolutionary Iranian committee trying to overthrow the current regime produced a fortnightly newsletter in Persian. In the old days, to circulate this in Iran would have been difficult, dangerous, and very uncertain in its results. When this group was formed some years ago, they just got a list of fax numbers, and they faxed their newsletter to every fax number they could find in Iran. Even if one assumes that most of the recipients destroyed it, one may be reasonably sure that they read it before doing so and may even have shared it with a friend or two. Now they don't even depend on fax; they have e-mail, Internet, and all the rest and latterly another immensely powerful weapon, satellite television. This is, of course, forbidden, and the young thugs of the *basīj* are sent out to destroy satellites. But the young thugs of the *basīj* also have a taste for seeing foreign television, and so they are bought off with seats from which they can watch the television performances, with the result that Iran is being flooded with all kinds of American television programs. I am told that the most popular by far at the present time is *Baywatch*. One may guess the cultural impact of that.

One other point may be worth making, in the comparison between Western types of democratic government and Middle Eastern types of authoritarian government. All forms of government and all types of regime are subject to the danger of corruption. No form of government has yet found a way of eliminating or totally avoiding corruption. But there is an interesting difference between democratic corruption and Middle Eastern corruption. In democratic corruption, you make money in the marketplace, and you use that money to buy power; in Middle Eastern corruption, you seize power and use the power to make money. From a moral or ethical point of view, I can see no difference between them; I cannot say that either one is better or worse than the other. But if we look at them from, shall we say, a political or economic point of view, I think we may agree that the Western form of corruption, though bad, does less damage to the polity or to the economy than the Middle Eastern form of corruption. In Israel, one sees an interesting compound, reflecting the mixed cultural heritage of the country, brought by Jews who came from both the Christian and Islamic worlds, and who brought some of the ways of those worlds with them.

Let me turn now to my second theme, which is legitimacy and, of course, closely connected with that, the question of succession, since in a legitimate government succession is according to accepted rules. By legitimacy, I mean a system in which the majority of the people accept the right of the ruler to rule. That's to say that they feel he is the rightful ruler, he is entitled to the authority he exercises, and he, on his side, does not need to use excessive force or brutality to maintain himself in power.

Under the old rules—and here it is more convenient to take legitimacy and succession together—succession was either hereditary, by nomination, or some combination of the two. By hereditary succession, I mean what normally one calls monarchy, though it seems to occur in other forms, too. In present-day Syria and Iraq, we have seen a new phenomenon unknown to history or political science: hereditary revolutionary leadership. I doubt if either Assad or Saddam ever used the term *monarchy* in relation to their appointment of their sons as their heirs, but obviously the trend was in that direction.

Here it might be useful to have a look at some common judgments regarding these systems. Three forms of governments have, generally speaking, been condemned by all right-minded, right-thinking people. The first is imperialism. We all agree, of course, that imperialism is a terrible thing: it is an outrage; it should be ended wherever it still exists and the people given their freedom. After the people of Hong Kong groaned for a hundred years under British tyranny, they now have found freedom in the bosom of mother China. I quote that example, which is by no means unique, to indicate that although imperialism obviously has a great many flaws and faults and is in many ways a destructive, disruptive force in history, there has also been a plus side in certain aspects, and I have more than once been assured by Egyptians, when no one else was around, that the period of British occupation was the freest in all their multimillennial history before and after.

Imperialism also sometimes leaves good as well as bad legacies. The British and French, who divided most of the Middle East between them, set up regimes in their own image. The British set up parliamentary monarchies, the French set up unstable republics. None of them seemed to have worked very well, although one of the monarchies still survives.

That brings me to the second of the unfashionable regimes, that of monarchy. Monarchy is not fashionable. In the United States in particular, the word *monarchy* is frequently used as the antithesis of democracy. If we look around the world, we must see that it is perfectly possible to have a monarchy that is democratic and to have a republic that is not democratic. Examples of both come readily to mind. Yet despite the contrasts between, say, Sweden and Libya, there is still a tendency to use *republic* and *democracy* as synonyms. In modern Greek, indeed, *demokratia* is the word for republic. Monarchy has certain benefits, not the least of which is a principle of succession that is recognized and accepted.

My third revisionist suggestion concerns military rule. I am sure we are all horrified at the idea that the soldiers step in, conduct a coup d'état, and take over. Yes, of course, this is terrible, and we must insist on an immediate return to democracy, even in a place where democracy has never previously existed.

But why does military rule happen? Consider the cases where there were, to use the Turkish term, military interventions. The Turks like to use the word *müdahele*, "intervention," rather than coup or takeover. *Müdahele* has a sort of clean, surgical connotation.

Why does it happen? It happens, usually speaking, when the regime is crumbling, when it's falling to pieces, in a situation where the army is only the institution in the state that still holds together, that still has some sort of command structure and some sort of hierarchy, and in which such words as *honor* and *loyalty* still retain some meaning. We may even accept that military takeovers in many cases have been motivated by the highest patriotic considerations. This is easy to believe if we look at some of the situations in which the military did take over.

The problem with this is that the army in politics inevitably means politics in the army, and that means that within usually quite a short time, the army becomes subject to the same degenerative processes as the civil society into which the army moved to take over. That is why in Turkey we see the unique phenomenon of a series of military interventions. The soldiers take over, they promise to go back to the barracks when they have made some order, nobody believes them, but in fact they do just that. They wait a little while, the democratic politicians mess it up again, and they do it for a second time, then a third time. The fourth one was described by a Turkish observer as "a postmodernist military intervention." This is a fairly good description of what happened when Necmettin Erbakan "resigned" from the office of prime minister in June 1997.

What do we see if we look around at the regimes in the present-day Middle East? There are monarchies in the full sense. Both Jordan and Morocco have recently passed the test of a smooth, untroubled succession. One important point: in the Western monarchies, the normal rule of succession was primogeniture—that is to say, the eldest son of the ruler succeeds him even if he is an infant, in which case there is a regency. But the rule was the succession of the oldest son, or where there is no son, in England, though not in France, it could be a daughter. In the British monarchy, daughters could succeed, and there were several very notable ones, Mary, Elizabeth, Anne, and of course Victoria and Her present Majesty. In France and most, but not all, of the continental monarchies, the succession of females was

excluded, which may be one reason why the British mon
still there and the others have gone.

In Middle Eastern monarchies, they never accep
principle of primogeniture. The general principle in
Eastern monarchies was nomination: the ruler nomina
successor-designate. It was not unusual—in fact, it w
frequent—for a sultan to be succeeded by a brother, a r
or even a cousin. That has an advantage in that it ensu
the successor is able to take over effectively. It has a di
tage in that it brings in an element of uncertainty, and
see a recent example of the sudden, last-minute chang
succession in the Kingdom of Jordan in February 19
might have caused trouble, but in fact it didn't. The syst
together.

Then we have the tribal monarchies, a term we can
Saudi Arabia and most of the Gulf States. These are not
chies in the sense that Morocco and Jordan are monarc
they are quasi-monarchical societies that seem to be
together for the time being, and in which succession is
less regulated along monarchical lines. Then there is
might call a nonhereditary monarchy, and there I
Egypt. In Egypt, the monarchy was abolished a long t
but we see a remarkable stability and continuity in tl
tian regime. Nasser died and was succeeded by hi
Sadat; Sadat was murdered and was succeeded by h:
Mubarak, and although Mubarak has not nominated
or successor, it seems likely that when he goes the v
flesh, unless there are radical changes in the meantim
be succeeded by someone else from the inner circle. T
tians have the advantage of a long-established, smoot
tioning centralized regime that in one sense goes b
than a century, and in another sense, several millenn
has a political class with considerable experience ir
control.

was long able to in the Soviet Union. In both branches of the Ba'athists, there was a movement toward monarchical succession in the party leadership and state dictatorship—successful in Syria, well-prepared but so far unsuccessful in Iraq.

How, then, do states in the Middle East determine succession? How have they done it in the past, how are they doing it now, and how are they likely to do it in the future? Basically, there are three methods. One is election, by which I mean genuine free election in the democratic style, that is to say, elections held at predetermined times in which the rules and opportunities are the same for all the contesting parties and in which the loser abides by the result. The second method, as we have seen, is nomination, normally but not necessarily hereditary. The third method of succession is by violence—assassination, coup d'état, insurrection, civil war, and similar methods of problem solving. We have no lack of examples of these in the history of the region, in parts of which they have even become what we might call norms.

What are the ideologies, the aspirations that have influenced the course of events I have just been describing, in the adoption, abandonment, formation, and transformation of institutions; the acceptance or rejection of legitimacy; and the determining of succession? For quite a long time now, there have been two dominant ideologies in most of the Middle East: nationalism and socialism. To these, one may add the bastard offspring of the two, national socialism, which has had a not inconsiderable impact in some countries. Today in virtually all the region, both nationalism and socialism are discredited—socialism by its failure, nationalism by its success. They are discredited and outdated. In 1945, the prestige of socialism was immense. In continental Europe, the Soviet Union had won a resounding military victory. In the British parliamentary election of that year, Churchill was defeated and replaced by a Labour government. Socialism of one sort or another seemed to be triumphant at both ends of Europe, and the impact of socialist ideas, policies, and programs of various sorts spread all over the Arab world. Today, they all look very tired, broken down, and ruined. Instead of bringing the promised freedom, they brought tyranny and subservience; instead of the promised prosperity, they brought poverty and misery. Socialist regimes all over the Middle East and North Africa are looking very, very bad.

So we find a mood of disillusionment. The old ideas just haven't worked. So what is one to do instead? A very striking feature of the Arab world today is that there is not a single Arab leader who commands any support outside his own country, as Nasser did, for example, in the great days of pan-Arabism, and even in their own countries, they need a considerable measure of force and repression to maintain themselves in power.

So what else is there in this mood of disillusionment, which is very clearly expressed in the media, in conversations, and everywhere else we look? Two main ideas compete at the present time in the Middle Eastern region, two diagnoses of the sickness of the society and two prescriptions for its cure. One of them is the modernist, usually secularist, approach, the idea that it is possible and necessary for the Islamic lands to become part of modern civilization; in other words, the region is backward and impoverished because it clings to outmoded ideas and institutions and that the remedy is to modernize. The once common term *Westernize* is no longer permitted, except in a negative sense, but in this perception *modernize* means much the same thing. This was the basic philosophy of the Turkish Republic, explicitly formulated by Kemal Atatürk and maintained in the Turkish Republic by those who regard themselves as his successors. There are increasing numbers in the hitherto tyrannized Arab countries who believe in that basic approach. For them, the remedy is modernization and, as an essential part of it, democratization. The holders of this view are becoming increasingly vocal and active.

The other is a quite different diagnosis. For them, what is wrong with the Islamic world is that Muslims have not been faithful to their inherited traditions; they have abandoned the true path, followed after alien ways, imitated the infidel, and allowed themselves to be influenced and led by others, and that is why their societies are sick and miserable. The remedy, of course, is a return to roots, to authentic Islam. One version of this is enthroned as the official ideology of the Islamic Republic of Iran. Another is that expressed in the manifesto and other writings of Osama bin Ladin and in various ways put into practice by al Qaeda. Here there is another element of danger. The Islamic Republic of Iran is Shi'ite and more militantly so since the election of 2005. Osama bin Ladin is militantly Sunni, as are his backers and followers in Saudi Arabia and elsewhere. There have been differences and indeed quarrels between Sunni and Shi'a, going back to the very beginnings of Islam, but in the past, they never reached the level of bitterness that provoked the intra-Christian religious wars and persecutions of Christendom, notably during and after the Reformation. There are disturbing signs of such a development in the Islamic world today.

The struggle continues even in Turkey and Iran. A significant proportion of the Turkish electorate voted in favor of an Islamic party, which has established an Islamic government. Its spokesmen claim that they are an Islamic democratic party, no different from the Christian democratic parties of Europe and equally at home in a democratic regime and society. Its critics accuse the government of trying to undermine the separation of religion and state that was fundamental to the Kemalist system and to bring about an Islamic restoration. Time will show. In Iran, we don't know what proportion of the electorate would vote for a secular regime; that option is not permitted in an Islamic theocracy. But from various signs, it is clear that the number is not inconsiderable.

Now the main center of struggle is in Iraq, where the attempt to create an Arab democracy has evoked powerful fears—in Europe and among some circles in America, that it won't work; in the Middle East, more urgently, that it will work and thus imperil the tyrants and autocrats who rule most of the countries of the region. This attempt to bring democracy to Iraq and elsewhere in the Arab world arouses powerful enemies: first, those who seek to preserve and reinforce the existing tyrannies by restoring the fallen tyranny of Saddam Hussein; and second, those whose declared aim is to destroy all these so-called Westernizing regimes and establish a universal Islamic theocracy, Sunni or Shi'ite.

There are obviously major differences of both policy and purpose, both between and within these various groups, but for the time being, they fight together against a common enemy— just as the democracies and the Soviets fought together against the Axis and resumed their conflict when the Axis was destroyed. They no doubt expect to do the same, if and when they achieve victory over the West in the present struggle.

The quintessential democratic instrument of legitimate succession is the election, and in this, the Iraqi election of January 2005 was a major occasion, even in the long history of that cradle of civilizations that we now call the Middle East. This election was an achievement first and foremost of the Iraqi people, who showed both wisdom and courage—wisdom in recognizing the meaning of freedom though it was unfamiliar and courage in operating it despite both danger and inexperience.

Sadly, many Iraqis are paying with their lives in the struggle to gain and retain freedom. For growing numbers of their compatriots, it is now the victims, not the perpetrators of terror they see, with mingled pride and compassion, as the martyrs and heroes of their cause. The Iraqis have made tremendous progress toward democracy, first by holding fair and contested elections and then by freely negotiating a series of compromise agreements to form a coalition government comprising diverse and even previously conflicting elements. In a country where freedom and compromise were equally unfamiliar, these are giant steps.

But another important step still remains. The underlying assumption of the Iraqi parties—and of some, at least, of their outside well-wishers and advisers—seems to be that to be part of a political process, one must somehow be part of the government. Failing that, one has no role in the political process, and one's only options are submission or resistance, the latter in the form of boycott, sabotage, terror, or armed insurrection.

This is a dangerous fallacy. There is another essential component of any democratic system, and that is a loyal, democratic opposition. The task of such an opposition is not to oppose the regime, though it may try, through democratic processes, to amend or modify its functioning. The task of a democratic opposition is to oppose the government, to strive to oust and replace it at the next election, and meanwhile to subject its actions, utterances, and policies to rigorous but fair scrutiny. The importance of an opposition is recognized even in some of the world's pseudo democracies, which adorn themselves with a tame, compliant pseudo opposition. That is not enough. The opposition must be real and free, with a genuine, equal chance of winning. Otherwise, the democratic process is about as meaningful as a football match with only one team.

In Britain, the traditional name for those who sit opposite the government benches in Parliament and thus on a daily basis confront and oppose them is "Her Majesty's loyal opposition." This term sometimes evokes derision or incomprehension in countries with different political traditions, but it expresses an important truth. In any functioning democracy, a loyal opposition is an essential component, and both the loyalty and the opposition must be authentic.

What is the role of what we proudly call the free world in this? No one can give, still less impose, freedom. But we can help to remove obstacles and especially help the peoples of the Middle East to get rid of the imported fascist ideology and apparatus of tyranny that suppressed and supplanted their own, older Islamic traditions of lawful, limited, and responsible government. These obstacles are still present in some countries in the region, and the rulers of those countries, mortally threatened by the irruption of freedom, will do all they can to stifle it.

The cause of freedom has won a major battle, but it has not yet won the war. Democracy in Iraq and elsewhere in the region faces a double threat, on the one hand from ruthless and resolute enemies and on the other from fickle and hesitant friends. We must stay with the Iraqi democrats, even if their choice of rulers is not what some of us would have preferred. It is their country, and freedom—a free election—means that the choice is theirs.

But our role has been, and will for a while remain, crucial. In successive phases, the free world enabled the peoples of Axis-ruled Europe and Asia to create or restore democracy. More recently, we helped give the peoples of the former Soviet bloc the opportunity to do the same, and some are well on the way. Now it is time for the countries of the Middle East to join the free world and recover their rightful place in the forefront of civilization.

TEN

The Relevance of History

Transcript: Organization of the Islamic Conference, European Union, France

L ET ME BEGIN BY EXPRESSING MY THANKS TO THE conveners of this meeting for giving me the opportunity to participate and the privilege of addressing you. Having said that, I feel I must follow with a word of confession and an apology. Unlike the vast majority of participants in this meeting, I am not in any way involved in the political process, neither as a politician, nor as a civil servant, nor even as a journalist. I speak to you as a historian, one who by profession deals with the past, marginally with the present, hardly at all with the future. Worse than that, I am a retired historian, so that even my past is, in a sense, passé. Nevertheless, I think history is something useful; indeed, I would go a step further and say essential. To contribute to this, I shall try to present history in a historical perspective rather than one of political, national, or sectarian disputation.

History is for society what memory is for the individual. Loss of memory we call amnesia, distorted memory we call neurosis, and the society that neglects its history or feeds itself on distorted history is an amnesiac or neurotic society. That is a dangerous situation for any society to be in.

Forgetting or distorting history is dangerous, and history has a tendency to reassert itself, sometimes rather suddenly and violently, as it did on September 11.

That brings a new danger: the danger of misreading, the danger of neglect, being now supplemented by the danger of exaggeration of one or other element in the situation. What September 11 brought was not a change in realities, which continue much as before, but a change in the common perception of those realities on all sides. We are here at a meeting of the OIC and of the European Union; that is to say, of the two bodies, at first sight, differently defined. One is defined by a shared religion, and indeed in the present world the only such international organization defined by religion. The other is defined ostensibly in geographical terms as a continent. But that continent was known, not so long ago, as Christendom, and obviously many still see it, perceive it, or feel it as the Christian world or, to use an increasingly common term, the post-Christian world. Between these two, there is a long historical relationship. And let us be frank and call things by their proper names, a long record of conflict. I don't want to go into a discussion of currently fashionable theories about the clash of civilizations. On that, let me just say this, that using the word *civilization* in the plural already marks considerable progress for most of us. In the common usage of humankind from remote antiquity until, shall we say, the day before yesterday, civilization meant us, and the rest were uncivilized. That we talk about civilizations in the plural is already a mark of progress and gives hope if we can manage to avoid the obvious pitfalls.

The long relationship between Christendom and Islam, between Europe and the Middle East, using the geographical terms, has mostly been one of conflict: the long series of wars that began in the seventh century with the advance of Muslim armies into the then Christian Byzantine territories, Syria, Egypt, Palestine, North Africa, and parts of Europe; the

European counterattack and attempted reconquest—the Crusades—new Muslim attacks from the Golden Horde to Russia, from the Ottoman Empire to Europe, and again the Christian counterattacks; the rival empires, the Ottomans reaching into the heart of Europe and later European empires reaching toward the heart of Islam. This is an ongoing process that has continued through most of the last of fourteen centuries. We shall be dangerously deluding ourselves if we pretend that it never happened and pretend that even if it did happen, it doesn't matter. It does matter.

But I think there is one very important point in this great debate, as the eighteenth-century English historian Gibbon called it. I prefer the word to *clash* between Christendom and Islam. And this really important point is that what divided them, what brought them into conflict, was not their differences but their resemblances. Christianity and Islam are both religions of very much the same kind with a common history, with common background and a large measure of common beliefs. When you have two religions with the same self-perceptions, making the same claims in the same geographical area, the conflict between them was virtually inevitable. But even so, there was a kind of unity in conflict. Christians and Muslims, right through the Middle Ages, could hold disputations. They could argue meaningfully and understand each other. When a Christian said to a Muslim or a Muslim said to a Christian, "You are an infidel, and you will burn in hell," each understood exactly what the other meant, because they both meant exactly the same thing. Their heavens are somewhat different, but their hells are practically identical. This kind of dialogue would have been meaningless between a Christian or a Muslim on the one side and a Buddhist or a Confucian on the other. There wasn't that measure of common heritage and common belief to make communication possible.

As the German historian Carl Heinrich Becker remarked early in the twentieth century, the real dividing line between East and West is not the dividing line between Christendom and Islam but the dividing line between Islam and what he called "the real Asia," which lies beyond. In these shared beliefs and these common aspirations, there is, I think, probably the best hope for future cooperation and understanding between them. And this becomes more and more possible with the growth of knowledge on both sides; as each learns more about the other, each gets to have a better understanding of the other. Now there are obvious difficulties in this, and there are obvious obstacles to this better understanding, but the thing I think give us most hope is that the basis of understanding in a common cultural and even religious heritage is there.

Now there are, of course, dangers. It is very easy to try to form unity between this continent and this religion on the basis of shared resentments and prejudices against other continents and other religions. Some would go a step further and try to assign to the European Union third place in succession to the Third Reich and the Soviet Union as the bastion of anti-Westernism and the patron of anti-Western causes—the West, of course, having meanwhile moved farther west across the Atlantic, from Western Europe to North America.

That is a danger, and one can understand that it could bring some immediate emotional satisfaction and perhaps even some temporary tactical advantage. But it is surely in the long run self-destructive for all concerned. What is surely much more important, much more valuable and practicable, is for the two to join forces against their real common enemies.

Both the Western and the Middle Eastern traditions agree in defining bad government as tyranny and oppression. They differ traditionally in defining good government. In the West, it has been defined as freedom; in the Islamic world, it has been defined as justice. The contrast is justice and tyranny as against the Western notion, freedom and tyranny. But increasingly justice and freedom are coming to mean the same thing. Now I think it is time to join forces against the common enemies—ignorance and bigotry, poverty and underdevelopment, tyranny and terror, so as to seek common benefits. And for all of these, both freedom and justice are essentials.

ELEVEN

Freedom and Justice in Islam

The following is adapted from a lecture delivered on 16 July 2006, on board the Crystal Serenity, *during a Hillsdale College cruise in the British Isles.*

B Y COMMON CONSENT AMONG HISTORIANS, THE modern history of the Middle East begins in the year 1798, when the French Revolution arrived in Egypt in the form of a small expeditionary force led by a young general called Napoleon Bonaparte—who conquered and then ruled it for a while with appalling ease. General Bonaparte—he wasn't yet emperor—proclaimed to the Egyptians that he had come to them on behalf of a French Republic built on the principles of liberty and equality. We know something about the reactions to this proclamation from the extensive literature of the Middle Eastern Arab world. The idea of equality posed no great problem. Equality is very basic in Islamic belief: all true believing men are equal. Of course, that still leaves three "inferior" categories of people—slaves, unbelievers, and women. But in general, the concept of equality was understood. Islam never developed anything like the caste system of India to the east or the privileged aristocracies of Christian Europe to the west. Equality was something they knew, respected, and in large measure practiced. But liberty was something else.

As used in Arabic at that time, liberty was not a political but a legal term: you were free if you were not a slave. The word *liberty* was not used as we use it in the Western world, as a metaphor for good government. So the idea of a republic founded on principles of freedom caused some puzzlement.

Some years later the Egyptian sheikh Rifāʿa Rāfi al Ṭahṭāwī, who went to Paris as chaplain to the first group of Egyptian students sent to Europe—wrote a book about his adventures and explained his discovery of the meaning of freedom. He wrote that when the French talk about freedom they mean what Muslims mean when they talk about justice. By equating freedom with justice, he opened a whole new phase in the political and public discourse of the Arab world and then, more broadly, the Islamic world.

IS WESTERN-STYLE FREEDOM TRANSFERABLE?

What is the possibility of freedom in the Islamic world, in the Western sense of the word? If you look at the current literature, you will find two views common in the United States and Europe. One of them holds that Islamic peoples are incapable of decent, civilized government. Whatever the West does, Muslims will be ruled by corrupt tyrants. Therefore, the aim of our foreign policy should be to ensure that they are *our* tyrants rather than someone else's—friendly rather than hostile tyrants. This point of view is very much favored in departments and ministries of foreign affairs and is generally known, rather surprisingly, as the "pro-Arab" view. It is, of course, in no sense pro-Arab. It shows ignorance of the Arab past, contempt for the Arab present, and unconcern for the Arab future. The second common view is that Arab ways are different from our ways. They must be allowed to develop in accordance with their cultural principles, but it is possible for them—as for anyone else, anywhere in the world, with discreet help from outside and most specifically from the United States—to develop democratic institutions of a kind. This view is known as the "imperialist" view and has been vigorously denounced and condemned as such.

In thinking about these two views, it is helpful to step back and consider what Arab and Islamic society was like once and how it has been transformed in the modern age. The idea that how that society is now is how it has always been is totally false. The dictatorship of Saddam Hussein in Iraq or the Assad family in Syria or the friendlier dictatorship of Mubarak in Egypt—all of these have no roots whatsoever in the Arab or Islamic past. Let me quote to you from a letter written in 1786—three years before the French Revolution—by Count de Choiseul-Gouffier, the French ambassador in Istanbul, in which he is trying to explain why he is making rather slow progress with the tasks entrusted to him by his government in dealing with the Ottoman government. "Here," he says, "things are not as in France where the king is sole master and does as he pleases." "Here," he says, "the sultan has to consult." He has to consult with the former holders of high offices, with the leaders of various groups, and so on. And this is a slow process. This scenario is something radically different than the common image of Middle Eastern government today. And it is a description that ceased to be true because of a number of changes that occurred.

MODERNIZATION AND NAZI AND SOVIET INFLUENCE

The first of these changes is what one might call modernization. This was undertaken not by imperialists, for the most part, but by Middle Eastern rulers who had become painfully aware that their societies were undeveloped compared with the advanced

Western world. These rulers decided that what they had to do was to modernize or Westernize. Their intentions were good, but the consequences were often disastrous. What they did was to increase the power of the state and the ruler enormously by placing at his disposal the whole modern apparatus of control, repression, and indoctrination. At the same time, which was even worse, they limited or destroyed those forces in the traditional society that had previously limited the autocracy of the ruler. In the traditional society, there were established orders—the bazaar merchants, the scribes, the guilds, the country gentry, the military establishment, the religious establishment, and so on. These were powerful groups in society, whose heads were not appointed by the ruler but arose from within the groups. And no sultan, however powerful, could do much without maintaining some relationship with these different orders in society. This is not democracy as we currently use that word, but it is certainly limited, responsible government. And the system worked. Modernization ended that. A new ruling class emerged, ruling from the center and using the apparatus of the state for its purposes.

That was the first stage in the destruction of the old order. The second stage we can date with precision. In the year 1940, the government of France surrendered to the Axis and formed a collaborationist government in a place called Vichy. The French colonial empire was, for the most part, beyond the reach of the Nazis, which meant that the governors of the French colonies had a free choice: to stay with Vichy or to join Charles de Gaulle, who had set up a Free French Committee in London. The overwhelming majority chose Vichy, which meant that Syria-Lebanon—a French-mandated territory in the heart of the Arab East—was now wide open to the Nazis. The governor and his high officials in the administration in Syria-Lebanon took their orders from Vichy, which in turn took orders from Berlin. The Nazis moved in, made a tremendous propaganda effort, and were even able to move from Syria eastward into Iraq and for a while set up a pro-Nazi, fascist regime. It was in this period that political parties were formed, that were the nucleus of what later became the Ba'th Party. The Western Allies eventually drove the Nazis out of the Middle East and suppressed these organizations. But the war ended in 1945, and the Allies left. A few years later, the Soviets moved in; established an immensely powerful presence in Egypt, Syria, Iraq, and various other countries; and introduced Soviet-style political practice. The adaptation from the Nazi model to the Communist model was very simple and easy, requiring only a few minor adjustments, and it proceeded pretty well. That is the origin of the Ba'th Party and of the kind of governments that we have been confronting in the Middle East in recent years. That, as I would again repeat and emphasize, has nothing whatever to do with the traditional Arab or Islamic past.

WAHHABISM AND OIL

That there has been a break with the past is a fact of which Arabs and Muslims themselves are keenly and painfully aware, and they have tried to do something about it. It is in this context that we observe a series of movements that could be described as an Islamic revival or reawakening. The first of these—founded by a theologian called Ibn 'Abd al-Wahhāb, who lived in a remote area of Najd in desert Arabia—is known as Wahhabi. Its argument is that the root of Arab-Islamic troubles lies in following the ways of the infidel. The Islamic world, it holds, has abandoned the true faith that God gave it through His prophet and His holy book, and the remedy is a return to pure, original Islam. This pure, original Islam is, of course—as is usual in such situations—a new invention with little connection to Islam as it existed in its earlier stages.

Wahhabism was dealt with fairly easily in its early years, but it acquired a new importance in the mid-1920s when two things happened: the local tribal chiefs of the House of Saud—who had been converted since the eighteenth century to the Wahhabi version of Islam—conquered the holy cities of Mecca and Medina. This was of immense importance, giving them huge prestige and influence in the whole Islamic world. It also gave them control of the pilgrimage, which brings millions of Muslims from the Islamic world together to the same place at the same time every year.

The other important thing that happened—also in the mid-1920s—was the discovery of oil. With that, this extremist sect found itself not only in possession of Mecca and Medina but also of wealth beyond the dreams of avarice. As a result, what would otherwise have been an extremist fringe in a marginal country became a major force in the world of Islam. And it has continued as a major force to the present day, operating through the Saudi government and through a whole series of non-governmental organizations. What is worse, its influence spreads far beyond the region. When Muslims living in Chicago or Los Angeles or Birmingham or Hamburg want to give their children some grounding in their faith and culture—a very natural, very normal thing—they turn to the traditional resources for such purposes: evening classes, weekend schools, holiday camps, and the like. The problem is that these are now overwhelmingly funded and therefore controlled by the Wahhabis, and the version of Islam that they teach is the Wahhabi version, which has thus become a major force in Muslim immigrant communities.

Let me illustrate the significance of this with one example: Germany has constitutional separation of church and state, but in the German school system, they provide time for religious instruction. The state, however, does not provide teachers or textbooks. They allow time in the school curriculum for the various churches and other religious communities—if they wish—to provide religious instruction to their children, which is entirely optional. The Muslims in Germany are mostly Turks. When they reached sufficient numbers, they applied to the German government for permission to teach Islam in German schools. The German authorities agreed, but said they—the Muslims—had to provide the teachers and the textbooks. The Turks said that they had excellent textbooks, which are used in Turkey and Turkish schools, but the German authorities said no, those are government-produced textbooks; under the principle of separation of church and state, these Muslims had to produce their own. As a result, whereas in Turkish schools in Turkey, students get a modern, moderate version of Islam, in German schools, in general, they get the full Wahhabi blast. The last time I looked, twelve Turks have been arrested as members of Al Qaeda—all twelve of them born and educated in Germany.

THE IRANIAN REVOLUTION AND AL QAEDA

In addition to the rising spread of Wahhabism, I would draw your attention to the Iranian Revolution of 1979. The word *revolution* is much misused in the Middle East; it is used for virtually every change of government. But the Iranian Revolution was a real revolution, in the sense that the French and Russian revolutions were real revolutions. It was a massive change in the country, a massive shift of power—socially, economically, and ideologically. And like the French and Russian revolutions in their prime, it also had a tremendous impact in the world with which the Iranians shared a common universe of discourse—the world of Islam. I remember not long after the Iranian Revolution I was visiting Indonesia where I had been invited to lecture in religious universities. I noticed in the student dorms they had pictures of Khomeini all over the place, although Khomeini—like the Iranians in general—is a Shi'ite, and the Indonesians are Sunnis. Indonesians generally showed little interest in what was happening in the Middle East. But this was something important. And the Iranian Revolution has gone through various familiar phases—familiar from the French and Russian revolutions—and its impact all over the Islamic world has been enormous.

The third and most recent phase of the Islamic revival is that associated with the name Al Qaeda—the organization headed by Osama bin Ladin. Here I would remind you of the events toward the end of the twentieth century: the defeat of the Russians in Afghanistan, the withdrawal of the defeated armies into Russia, the collapse and breakdown of the Soviet Union. We are accustomed to regard that as a Western or, more specifically, an American victory in the Cold War. In the Islamic world, it was nothing of the kind. It was Muslim victory in a jihad. And if we are fair about it, we must admit that this interpretation of what happened does not lack plausibility. In the mountains of Afghanistan, which the Soviets had conquered and had been trying to rule, the Taliban were able to inflict one defeat after another on the Soviet forces, eventually driving the Red Army out of the country to defeat and collapse.

Thanks to modern communications and the modern media, we are quite well informed about how Al Qaeda perceives things. Osama bin Ladin is very articulate, very lucid, and I think on the whole very honest in the way he explains things. As he sees it, and as his followers see it, there has been an ongoing struggle between the two world religions—Christianity and Islam—which began with the advent of Islam in the seventh century and has been going on ever since. The Crusades were one aspect, but there were many others. It is an ongoing struggle of attack and counter attack, conquest and reconquest, jihad and Crusade, ending, so it seems, in a final victory of the West with the defeat of the Ottoman Empire—the last of the great Muslim states—and the partition of most of the Muslim world between the Western powers. As Osama bin Ladin puts it: "In this final phase of the ongoing struggle, the world of the infidels was divided between two superpowers—the United States and the Soviet Union. Now we have defeated and destroyed the more difficult and the more dangerous of the two. Dealing with the pampered and effeminate Americans will be easy." And then followed what has become the familiar description of the Americans and the usual litany and recitation of American defeats and retreats: Vietnam, Beirut, Somalia, one after another. The general theme was: They can't take it. Hit them and they'll run. All you have to do is hit harder. This seemed to receive final confirmation during the 1990s, when one attack after another on embassies, warships, and barracks brought no response beyond angry words and expensive missiles misdirected to remote and uninhabited places, and in some places—as in Beirut and Somalia—prompt retreats.

What happened on 9/11 was seen by its perpetrators and sponsors as the culmination of the previous phase and the inauguration of the next phase—taking the war into the enemy camp to achieve final victory. The response to 9/11 came as a nasty surprise. They were expecting more of the same— bleating and apologies—instead of which they got a vigorous reaction, first in Afghanistan and then in Iraq. And as they used to say in Moscow: it is no accident, comrades, that there has been no successful attack in the United States since then. But if one follows the discourse, one can see that the debate in this country since then has caused many of the perpetrators and sponsors to return to their previous diagnosis. Because remember, they have no experience, and therefore no understanding, of the free debate of an open society. What we see as free debate, they see as weakness, fear, and division. Thus they prepare for the final victory, the final triumph and the final jihad.

CONCLUSION

There are, as I've tried to point out, elements in Islamic society that could well be conducive to democracy. And there are encouraging signs at the present moment—what happened in Iraq, for example, with millions of Iraqis willing to stand in line to vote, knowing that they were risking their lives, is a quite extraordinary achievement. It shows great courage, great resolution. Don't be misled by what you read in the media about Iraq. The situation is certainly not good, but there are redeeming features in it. The battle isn't over. It's still very difficult. There are still many major problems to overcome. There is a bitter anti-Western feeling that derives partly and increasingly from our support for what they see as tyrannies ruling over them. It's interesting that pro-American feeling is strongest in countries with anti-American governments. I've been told repeatedly by Iranians that there is no country in the world where pro-American feeling is stronger, deeper, and more widespread than Iran. I've heard this from so many different Iranians—including some still living in Iran—that I believe it. When the American planes were flying over Afghanistan, the story was that many Iranians put signs on their roofs in English reading, "This way, please."

So there is a good deal of pro-Western and even specifically pro-American feeling. But the anti-American feeling is strongest in those countries that are ruled by what we are pleased to call "friendly governments." And it is those, of course, that are the most tyrannical and the most resented by their own people. The outlook at the moment is, I would say, very mixed. I think that the cause of developing free institutions—along their lines, not ours—is possible. One can see signs of its beginning in some countries. At the same time, the forces working against it are very powerful and well entrenched. And one of the greatest dangers is that on their side, they are firm and convinced and resolute, whereas on *our* side, we are weak and undecided and irresolute. And in such a combat, it is not difficult to see which side will prevail.

I think that the effort is difficult and the outcome uncertain, but I think the effort must be made. Either we bring them freedom, or they destroy us.

TWELVE

Europe and Islam

I T IS SOMETIMES FORGOTTEN THAT THE CONTENT OF history—the business of the historian—is the past, not the future. I remember being at an international meeting of historians in Rome during which a group of us were sitting and discussing the question: should historians attempt to predict the future? We batted this back and forth, with differing, even contrasting responses. This was in the days when the Soviet Union was still alive and well. One of our Soviet colleagues finally intervened and said, "In the Soviet Union, the most difficult task of the historian is to predict the past."

I do not intend to offer any predictions of the future of Europe or of Islam, but one thing can legitimately be expected of the historian, and that is to identify trends and processes—to look at trends in the past, at what is continuing in the present, and therefore to see the possibilities and choices that will face us in the future.

In dealing with the Islamic world, there is a special reason for paying attention to history—that this is a society of unusually keen historical awareness. Unlike what is happening in America and, to an increasing extent, Europe, in the Islamic lands, and especially in the Middle East, historical knowledge, back to the advent of Islam in the seventh century, is widespread, extensive, and, if not always accurate, both vivid and detailed. During the war fought from 1980 to 1988 between two Muslim powers, Iraq and Iran, the war propaganda of both sides, addressed both to their own people and to the enemy, was full of allusions to history—not stories told from history, but rapid, passing allusions, sometimes no more than the name of a person or a place or an event. These were used in the sure knowledge that they would be picked up and understood, even by that significant part of the intended audience that was illiterate. Many of the allusions referred to events of the seventh century of the Common Era—events that are still vividly remembered and deeply significant. Some knowledge of history is essential if one is to understand the public discourse of Muslim leaders at the present time—both at home and in exile, both in government and in opposition.

A favorite theme of the historian is periodization—dividing history into periods. Periodization is mostly a convenience of the historian for purposes of writing or teaching. Nevertheless, there are times in the long history of the human adventure when we have a real turning point, a major change—the end of an era, the beginning of a new era. I am becoming more and more convinced that we are in such an age at the present time—a change in history comparable with the fall of Rome, the advent of Islam, and the discovery of America.

Conventionally, the modern history of the Middle East begins at the end of the eighteenth century, when a small French expeditionary force commanded by a young general called Napoleon Bonaparte was able to conquer Egypt and rule it with impunity. It was a terrible shock that one of the heartlands of Islam could be invaded and occupied with virtually no effective resistance. The second shock came a few years later with the departure of the French, which was brought about not by the Egyptians nor by their suzerains, the Ottoman Turks, but by a small squadron of the British Royal Navy commanded by a young admiral called Horatio Nelson, who drove the French out of Egypt and back to France.

Those events were of profound symbolic importance. From the beginning of the nineteenth century onward, the heartlands of Islam were no longer wholly controlled by the rulers of Islam. They were under direct or indirect influence or, more frequently, control from outside, from different parts of Europe or, as they saw it, Christendom. It was only then that the previously unknown name "Europe" began to be used in the Muslim Middle East—a change of terminology more than of connotation.

The dominant forces in the lands of the Muslims were now outside forces. What shaped their lives were foreign actions and decisions. What gave them choices were foreign rivalries. The political game that they could play—the only one that was open to them—was to try to profit from the rivalries between the outside powers, to try to use them against one another. We see that again and again in the course of the nineteenth and twentieth and even into the beginning of the twenty-first century. We see, for example, in the First World War, the Second World War, and the Cold War how Middle Eastern leaders played this game with varying degrees of success.

For a long time, the contenders competing for domination were the rival European imperial powers—Britain, France, Germany, Russia, Italy. In the final phase in the twentieth century, these rivalries acquired an explicit ideological content—in World War II, the Allies versus the Axis; in the Cold War, the West versus the Soviets. On the principle of "the enemy of my enemy is my friend," it was natural for people under foreign rule or domination to turn to the imperial—and later, also ideological—rivals of their masters. Pro-Nazi and later pro-Soviet factions, with sometimes the same leaders, among the subject peoples of the British and French empires illustrate this well. Interestingly, there seem to have been no corresponding pro-Western movements among the Muslim peoples subject to Soviet rule. The Soviets, even on the eve of their collapse, were much more adept at both indoctrination and repression than the more open empires of the West.

That game is now over. The era that was inaugurated by Napoleon and Nelson was terminated by Reagan and Gorbachev. The Middle East is no longer ruled or dominated by outside powers. Middle Easterners are having some difficulty in adjusting to this new situation, in taking responsibility for their own actions and their consequences. I remember being asked by an Iranian lady, bitterly critical of the government in her country, why "the imperialist powers had decided to impose an Islamist theocratic regime on Iran." But some are beginning to take responsibility now, and this change has been expressed with his usual clarity and eloquence by Osama bin Ladin.

☙

With the ending of the era of outside domination, we see the reemergence of certain older trends and deeper currents in Middle Eastern history, which had been submerged or at least obscured during the centuries of Western domination. Now they are coming back again. One trend consists of the internal struggles—ethnic, sectarian, regional—between different forces within the Middle East. These had of course continued but were of less importance in the imperialist era. Now they are coming out again and gaining force, as we see from the current clash between Sunni and Shī'a Islam, on a scale without precedent for centuries.

Another change more directly relevant to our present theme is the return among Muslims to what they perceive as the cosmic struggle between the two main faiths, Christianity and Islam. There are many religions in the world, but as far as I know there are only two that have claimed that their truths are not only universal (all religions claim that) but also exclusive: that they—the Christians in the one case, the Muslims in the other—are the privileged recipients of God's final message to humanity, which it is their duty not to keep selfishly to themselves, like the followers of ethnic or regional cults, but to bring to the rest of humanity, removing whatever obstacles there may be on the way. This self-perception, shared between Christendom and Islam, led to the long struggle that has been going on for more than fourteen centuries and is now entering a new phase. In the Christian world, now at the beginning of the twenty-first century of its era, this triumphalist attitude no longer prevails and is confined to a few minority groups. In the world of Islam, now in its early fifteenth century, triumphalism is still a significant force and has found expression in new militant movements.

It is interesting that in earlier times, both sides for quite a long time refused to recognize this as a struggle between religions—that is, to recognize the other as a rival universal religion. They saw it rather as between religion—meaning their own true faith—and the unbelievers or infidels (in Arabic, *kāfir*). Both sides long preferred to name each other by nonreligious terms. The Christian world called the Muslims Moors, Saracens, Tatars, and Turks; even a convert was said to have "turned Turk." The Muslims for their part called those they met in the Christian world Romans, Franks, Slavs, and the like. It was only slowly and reluctantly that they began to give each other religious designations, and then these were for the most part inaccurate and demeaning. In the West, it was customary to call Muslims Mohammadans, which they never called themselves; this was based on the totally false assumption that Muslims worship Muhammad in the way that Christians worship Christ. The usual Muslim term for Christians was Nazarene—*naṣrānī*—implying the local cult of a place called Nazareth.

The declaration of war came almost at the very beginning of Islam. According to an early story, in the year 7 of the Hegira, corresponding to 628 C.E., the Prophet sent six messengers, with letters, to the Byzantine and Persian emperors, the Negus of Ethiopia, and other rulers and princes, informing them of his advent and summoning them to embrace his faith or suffer the consequences. The authenticity of these prophetic letters is doubted, but their message is accurate in the sense that it does reflect a view dominant among Muslims since early times.

A little later we have hard evidence—and I mean hard in the most literal sense—in inscriptions. One of the famous sights of Jerusalem is a remarkable building known as the Dome of the Rock. It is in several ways significant. It is built on the Temple Mount, a place sacred to the Judeo-Christian tradition. Its architectural style is that of the earliest Christian churches. The oldest Muslim religious building outside Arabia, it dates from the end of the seventh century and was built by 'Abd al-Malik, one of the early caliphs. Specially significant is the message in the inscriptions on the building: "He is God, He is one, He has no companion, He does not beget, He is not begotten" (*Qur'ān*, IX, 31-3; CXII, 1-3). This is clearly a direct challenge to certain central principles of the Christian faith.

Interestingly, the caliph proclaimed the same message with a new gold coinage. Until then, striking gold coins had been an exclusive Roman, later Byzantine prerogative, and other states, including the Islamic caliphate, imported them as required. The Islamic caliph for the first time struck gold coins, breaching the immemorial privilege of Rome and putting the same inscription on them. The Byzantine emperor understood the double challenge, and went to war—without effect.

The Muslim attack on Christendom and the resulting conflict, which arose more from their resemblances than from their differences, has so far gone through three phases. The first dates from the very beginning of Islam, when the new faith spilled out of the Arabian Peninsula, where it was born, into the Middle East and beyond. It was then that Muslim armies from Arabia conquered Syria, Palestine, Egypt, and North Africa—all at that time part of the Christian world—and began the process of Islamization and Arabization. From there they advanced into Europe, conquering Spain, Portugal, Sicily, and the adjoining regions of mainland southern Italy, all of which became part of the Islamic world, and even crossing the Pyrenees and for a while occupying parts of France.

After a long and bitter struggle, the Christians managed to retake some but not all of the territories they had lost. They succeeded in Europe, and in a sense Europe was defined by the limits of their success. They failed to retake North Africa or the Middle East, which were lost to Christendom. Notably, they failed to recapture the Holy Land, in the series of campaigns known as the Crusades.

That was not the end of the matter. In the meantime the Islamic world, having failed to conquer Europe the first time, was moving toward a second attack, this time conducted not by Arabs and Moors but by Turks and Tatars. In the mid-thirteenth century the Mongol conquerors of Russia were converted to Islam. The Turks, who had already conquered hitherto Christian Asia Minor, advanced into Europe and in 1453 captured the ancient Christian city of Constantinople. They conquered the Balkans and for a while ruled half of Hungary. Twice they reached as far as Vienna, to which they laid siege in 1529 and again in 1683. Barbary corsairs from North Africa—well-known to historians of the United States—were raiding Western Europe. They went to Iceland—the uttermost limit—in 1627 and to several places in Western Europe.

Again, Europe counterattacked, this time more successfully and more rapidly. The Christians succeeded in recovering Russia and the Balkan Peninsula, and in advancing further into the Islamic lands, chasing their former rulers whence they had come. For this phase of European counterattack, a new term was invented: imperialism. When the peoples of Asia and Africa invaded Europe, this was not imperialism. When Europe attacked Asia and Africa, it was. This notion served as a double source of inspiration—of resentment for the one side, of guilt for the other. The West, no doubt because of its Judeo-Christian heritage, has a long tradition of guilt and self-flagellation. Imperialism, sexism, and racism are all Western terms, not because the West invented them—they are part of our common human and perhaps also animal heritage—but because the West was the first to identify, name, and condemn them and to wage a struggle against them, with some measure of success.

This European counterattack began a new phase, which brought European rule into the very heart of the Middle East. It was completed in the aftermath of World War I; it was ended in the aftermath of World War II. In our own time, we have seen the end of European, including Russian, domination in the lands of Islam.

Osama bin Ladin, in some very interesting proclamations and declarations, gives his view of the 1978–88 war in Afghanistan, which, it will be recalled, led to the defeat and retreat of the Red Army and the collapse of the Soviet Union. We tend to see that as a Western victory, more specifically an American victory, in the Cold War against the Soviets. For Osama bin Ladin, it was nothing of the kind. It was a Muslim victory in a jihad against the infidels. If one looks at what happened in Afghanistan and what followed, this is a not implausible interpretation.

As Osama bin Ladin saw it, Islam had reached its ultimate humiliation in this long struggle in the period after World War I—when the last of the great Muslim empires, the Ottoman Empire, was broken up and most of its territories divided between the victorious allies, and when the caliphate was suppressed and abolished and the last caliph driven into exile by secular, Westernizing Turks. This seemed to be the lowest point in Muslim history.

In his perception, the millennial struggle between the true believers and the unbelievers had gone through successive phases, in which the former were headed by various dynasties of caliphs, and the latter by the various imperial Christian powers that had succeeded the Romans in the leadership of the world of the infidels—the Byzantine Empire, the Holy Roman Empire, the British and French and Russian empires. In this final phase, he says, the world of the infidels was divided and disputed between two rival superpowers, the United States and the Soviet Union. The Muslims had met, defeated, and destroyed the more dangerous and the more deadly of the two. Dealing with the soft, pampered, and effeminate Americans would be an easy matter.

This belief appeared to be confirmed in the 1990s when the world saw one attack after another on American bases and installations with virtually no effective response of any kind—only angry words and expensive missiles dispatched to remote and uninhabited places. The lessons of Vietnam and Beirut (1983) were confirmed by Mogadishu (1993). In both Beirut and Mogadishu, a murderous attack on Americans, who were there as part of U.N.–sponsored missions, was followed by prompt and complete withdrawal. The message was understood and explained. "Hit them, and they'll run." This was the course of events leading up to 9/11. That attack was clearly intended to be the completion of the first sequence and the beginning of the new one, taking the war into the heart of the enemy camp.

∾

In the eyes of a fanatical and resolute minority of Muslims, the third wave of attack on Europe has clearly begun. We should not delude ourselves as to what it is and what it means. This time it is taking different forms and two in particular: terror and migration.

Terror is part of the larger issue of violence and of its use in the cause of religion. Islam does not, as some would have us believe, share the pacifist aspirations of early Christianity. Islamic theology and law—like Christian practice if not theory—recognize war as a fact of life and in certain situations commend and even require it. In the traditional view, the world is divided into two—the House of Islam where Islamic rule and law prevail, and the rest, known as the Dār al-Ḥarb, the House of War. Later, for a while, some intermediate categories were introduced to designate regimes with limited autonomy under Muslim suzerainty.

War does not mean terror. Islamic teachings, and more specifically Islamic law, regulate the conduct of warfare, requiring respect for the laws of war and humane treatment of women, children, and other noncombatants. They do not countenance actions of the type now designated as terrorism. Islamic doctrine and law forbid suicide, which is regarded as a major sin, earning eternal damnation. The suicide, according to Islamic teaching, even if he has lived a life of unremitting virtue, will forfeit paradise and will go to hell, where his punishment will consist of the eternal repetition of the act by which he committed suicide.

These rules and beliefs were generally respected in classical Islamic times. They have been eroded, reinterpreted, and explained away by the various schools of present-day radical Islam. The young men and women who commit these acts of terror should be better informed of the doctrines and traditions of their own faith. Unfortunately, they are not; instead, the suicide bomber and other kinds of terrorists have become role models, eagerly followed by growing numbers of frustrated and angry young men and women.

The other form, of more immediate relevance to Europe, is migration. In earlier times, it was inconceivable that a Muslim would voluntarily move to a non-Muslim country. The jurists discuss the question of a Muslim living under non-Muslim rule in the textbooks and manuals of Sharī'a but in a different form: Is it permissible for a Muslim to live in or even visit a non-Muslim country? And if he does, what must he do? Generally speaking, this was considered under certain specific headings.

The first case is that of a captive or a prisoner of war. Obviously, he has no choice, but he must preserve his faith and return home as soon as possible.

The second case is that of an unbeliever in the land of the unbelievers who sees the light and embraces the true faith—in other words, becomes a Muslim. He must leave as soon as possible and go to a Muslim country.

The third case is that of a visitor. For a long time, the only purpose that was considered legitimate was to ransom captives. This was later expanded into diplomatic and commercial missions.

With the advance of the European counterattack, there was a new issue in this ongoing debate. What is the position of a Muslim if his country is conquered by infidels? May he stay or must he leave?

We have some interesting discussions of these questions, after the Norman conquest of Muslim Sicily in the eleventh century, and especially from the late fifteenth century, when the reconquest of Spain was completed and Moroccan jurists were discussing this question. They asked if Muslims might stay. The general answer was no, they may not. The question was asked: May they stay if the Christian government that takes over is tolerant? (This proved to be a purely hypothetical question, of course.) The answer was still no; even then they may not stay, because the temptation to apostasy would be even greater. They must leave and hope that in God's good time they will be able to reconquer their homelands and restore the true faith.

This was the line taken by most jurists. There were some, at first a minority, later a more important group, who said that it is permissible for Muslims to stay provided certain conditions are met, mainly that they are allowed to practice their faith. This raises another question: what is meant by practicing their faith? Here we must remember that we are dealing not only with a different religion but also with a different concept of what religion is about, especially in regard to the Sharī'a, the holy law of Islam, covering a wide range of matters regarded as secular in the Christian world even during the medieval period, and certainly in what some call the post-Christian era of the Western world.

All of these discussions relate to the problems of a Muslim who, for one reason or another, finds himself under infidel rule. The one possibility that, it seems, never entered the minds of the classical jurists was that a Muslim might, of his own free will, leave the House of Islam and go to live, permanently, in an infidel land, the House of War, under infidel rule. But this is what has been happening, on an ever increasing scale, in recent and current times.

There are obviously now many attractions that draw Muslims to Europe, particularly in view of the growing economic impoverishment of much of the Muslim world and the worsening rapacity and tyranny of many of its rulers. Europe offers opportunities for employment and benefits even for unemployment. Muslim immigrants also enjoy freedom of expression and levels of education they lack at home. Even terrorists have far greater freedom of preparation and operation in Europe—and to a degree also in America—than they do in most Islamic lands.

There are some other factors of importance in the situation at this moment. One is the new radicalism in the Islamic world, which comes in several kinds: Sunni, especially Wahhābī, and Iranian Shi'ite, dating from the Iranian revolution. Both of these are becoming enormously important factors. We have the strange paradox that the danger of Islamic radicalism or of radical terrorism is far greater in Europe and America than it is in most of the Middle East and North Africa, where rulers are more skilled and less inhibited in controlling their extremists than are Westerners. Nevertheless, growing numbers of Muslims are beginning to see Islamic radicalism as a greater danger to Islam than to the West.

The Sunni kind is mainly Wahhābī, a radical version of Islam that first appeared in the remote district of Najd in Arabia in the eighteenth century. Among the converts to Wahhabism were the House of Saud, the local tribal chiefs. With the Saudi conquest of the Hijaz in the mid-1920s and the formation of the Saudi Arabian Kingdom, what was previously an extremist fringe in a marginal country became a major force in all the lands of Islam and beyond. Wahhabism has benefited greatly from the prestige, influence, and power of the House of Saud as controllers of the holy places of Islam, of the annual pilgrimage, and of the enormous wealth that oil has placed at their disposal.

The Iranian revolution is something different. The term *revolution* is much used in the Middle East. It is virtually the only generally accepted title of legitimacy. But the Iranian revolution was a real revolution in the sense in which we use that term of the French and Russian revolutions. Like the French and Russian revolutions in their day, it has had an enormous impact in the whole area with which the Iranians share a common universe of discourse—that is to say, in the entire Islamic world, Shī'a and Sunni, in the Middle East and far beyond.

Another question much discussed nowadays is that of assimilation. How far is it possible for Muslim migrants who have settled in Europe, in North America, and elsewhere to become part of the countries in which they settle, in the way that so many other waves of immigrants have done?

There are several points that need to be considered. One of them is the basic differences in what precisely is intended and understood by assimilation. Here there is an immediate and obvious contrast between the European and the American situations. For an immigrant to become an American means a change of political allegiance. For an immigrant to become a Frenchman or a German means a change of ethnic identity. Changing political allegiance is certainly easier and more practical than changing ethnic identity, either in one's own feelings or in one's measure of acceptance. For a long time, England had it both ways. A naturalized immigrant became British but did not become English.

I mentioned earlier the important difference in what one means by religion. For Muslims, it covers a whole range of different things, usually designated as the laws of personal status; marriage, divorce, and inheritance are the most obvious examples. Since antiquity, in the Western world many of these have been secular matters. The distinction between church and state, spiritual and temporal, ecclesiastical and lay, is a Christian concept that has no place in Islamic history and therefore is difficult to explain to Muslims, even at the present day. Until modern times they did not even have a vocabulary to express it. They have one now.

What are the European responses to this situation? In Europe, as in the United States, a frequent response is what is variously known as multiculturalism and political correctness. In the Muslim world there are no such inhibitions. They are very conscious of their identity. They know who they are and what they want, a quality that many in the West seem to a very large extent to have lost. This is a source of strength in the one, of weakness in the other.

Another popular Western response is what is sometimes called constructive engagement—"*Let's talk to them, let's get together and see what we can do.*" This approach dates back to early times. When Saladin reconquered Jerusalem and other places in the Holy Land, he allowed the Christian merchants from Europe to stay in the seaports where they had established themselves under Crusader rule. He apparently felt the need to justify this, and he wrote a letter to the caliph in Baghdad explaining his action. The merchants, he said, were useful since "there is not one among them that does not bring and sell us weapons of war, to their detriment and to our advantage." This continued during the Crusades and after. Even as the Ottoman armies were advancing into the heart of Europe, they could always find European merchants willing to sell them weapons, and European bankers willing to finance their purchases. The modern purveyors of advanced weaponry to Saddam Hussein yesterday and to the rulers of Iran today continue the tradition. Constructive engagement has a long history.

Contemporary attempts at dialogue also take other forms. We have seen in our own day the extraordinary spectacle of a pope apologizing to the Muslims for the Crusades. I would not wish to defend the behavior of the Crusaders, which was in many respects atrocious. But let us have a little sense of proportion. We are now expected to believe that the Crusades were an unwarranted act of aggression against a peaceful Muslim world. Hardly. The first papal call for a crusade occurred in 846 C.E., when a naval expedition from Arab-ruled Sicily, estimated by contemporaries at seventy-three ships and ten thousand men, sailed up the Tiber and attacked Rome. They briefly seized Ostia and Porto, and plundered St. Peter's Basilica in Rome and St. Paul's Cathedral on the right bank of the Tiber. In response, a synod in France issued an appeal to Christian sovereigns to rally against "the enemies of Christ," and the Pope, Leo IV, offered a heavenly reward to those who died fighting the Muslims—less specific than the Muslim promise of which it was probably a reflection. It is common practice in war to learn from the enemy and, when feasible, to adopt his more effective devices.

Two-and-a-half centuries and many battles later, in 1096, the Crusaders actually arrived in the Middle East. The Crusades were a late, limited, and unsuccessful imitation of the jihad—an attempt to recover by holy war what had been lost by holy war. It failed, and it was not followed up.

A striking example of the modern approach comes from France. On October 8, 2002, the then–prime minister, Monsieur Jean-Pierre Raffarin, made a speech in the French National Assembly discussing the situation in Iraq. Speaking of Saddam Hussein, he remarked that one of Saddam Hussein's heroes was his compatriot Saladin, who came from the same Iraqi town of Tikrit. In case the members of the Assembly were not aware of Saladin's identity, M. Raffarin explained to them that it was he who was able "to defeat the Crusaders and liberate Jerusalem." When a Catholic French prime minister describes Saladin's capture of Jerusalem from the largely French Crusaders as an act of liberation, this would seem to indicate a rather extreme case of realignment of loyalties or at least of perceptions. According to the parliamentary record, when M. Raffarin used the word *liberate*, a member called out, "Libérer?" The prime minister just went straight on. That was the only interruption, and as far as I know there was no comment afterward.

The Islamic radicals have even been able to find some allies in Europe. In describing them I shall have to use the terms *left* and *right*, terms which are becoming increasingly misleading. The seating arrangements in the first French National Assembly after the revolution are not the laws of nature, but we have become accustomed to using them. They are often confusing when applied to the West nowadays. They are utter nonsense when applied to different brands of radical Islam. But they are what people use, so let us put it this way.

The radical Islamists have a left-wing appeal to the anti-American elements in Europe, for whom they have replaced the Soviets. They have a right-wing appeal to the anti-Jewish elements in Europe, replacing the Nazis. They have been able to win considerable support under both headings, often from the same people. For some in Europe, hatreds apparently outweigh loyalties.

There is an interesting variation in Germany, where the Muslims are mostly Turkish. There they have often tended to equate themselves with the Jews, to see themselves as having succeeded the Jews as the victims of German racism and persecution. I remember a meeting in Berlin convened to discuss the new Muslim minorities in Europe. In the evening I was asked by a group of Turkish Muslims to join them and hear what they had to say about it, which was very interesting. The phrase which sticks most vividly in my mind from one of them was, "In a thousand years they [the Germans] were unable to accept 400,000 Jews. What hope is there that they will accept two million Turks?" They sometimes use this line, playing on German feelings of guilt, to advance their own agenda.

This raises the larger question of toleration. At the completion of the first phase of the Christian reconquest in Spain and Portugal, Muslims—who by that time were very numerous in the reconquered lands—were given a choice: baptism. exile, or death. In the former Ottoman lands in southeastern Europe, the leaders of what one might call the second reconquest were somewhat more tolerant, but not a great deal more. Some Muslim populations remain in the Balkan countries, with troubles still going on at the present day. Kosovo and Bosnia are the best known examples.

The question of religious tolerance raises new and important issues. In the past, during the long struggles between Muslims and Christians in both eastern and western Europe, there could be little doubt that the Muslims were far more tolerant, both of other religions and of diversity within their own religion, than were the Christians. In medieval Western Christendom, massacres and expulsions, inquisitions and immolations were commonplace; in Islam they were atypical and rare. The movement of refugees at that time was overwhelmingly from West to East and not, as in later times, from East to West. True, non-Muslim subjects in a Muslim state were subject to certain disabilities, but their situation was vastly better than that of unbelievers and misbelievers in Christian Europe.

These disabilities, acceptable in the past, came increasingly into conflict with democratic notions of civilized coexistence. Already in 1689, the English philosopher John Locke, in his *Letters Concerning Toleration*, remarked that "neither Pagan, nor Mahometan, nor Jew, ought to be excluded from the civil rights of the commonwealth because of his religion." In 1790, George Washington, in a letter to a Jewish community leader in Newport, Rhode Island, went even further, and dismissed the very idea of toleration as essentially intolerant, "as if it was by the indulgence of one class of people that another enjoyed the exercise of their inherent natural rights."

By the late seventeenth century, the practical situation was much better in Western Europe than in the Islamic lands. And from that time onward the one got better, the other got worse. Discrimination and persecution did not disappear in the West but, with the glaring exception of the Nazi interlude in continental Europe, the situation of religious minorities was better in the confident, advancing West than in the threatened, retreating East.

Muslims, and also many of their non-Muslim compatriots, did not see it that way, but thought of toleration in somewhat different terms. When Muslim immigrants came to live in Europe, they had a certain expectation, a feeling that they were entitled to at least the degree of toleration they had accorded to non-Muslims in the great Muslim empires of the past. Both their expectations and their experience were very different.

Coming to European countries, they got both more and less than they had expected: more in the sense that they got in theory and often in practice equal political rights, equal access to the professions, welfare, freedom of expression, and other benefits.

But they also got significantly less than they had given in traditional Islamic states. In the Ottoman Empire and other states before that—I mention the Ottoman Empire as the most recent—the non-Muslim communities had separate organizations and ran their own affairs. They collected their own taxes and enforced their own laws. There were several Christian communities, each living under its own leadership, recognized by the state. These communities ran their own schools and their own education systems and administered their own laws in such matters as marriage, divorce, and inheritance, as well as religious observance. The Jews did the same.

So you had a situation in which three men living in the same street could die and their estates would be distributed under three different legal systems if one of them happened to be Jewish, one Christian, and one Muslim. A Jew could be punished by a rabbinical court and jailed for violating the Sabbath or eating on Yom Kippur. A Christian could be arrested and imprisoned for taking a second wife. Bigamy is a Christian offense; it was not an Islamic or an Ottoman offense. By similar reasoning, Jews and Christians were exempt from the distinctively Islamic rules. They were allowed to eat, even in public, during the sacred month of Ramadan. They were permitted to make, sell, serve, and drink wine, as long as they did all these things among themselves. Some documents in the Ottoman archives discuss a problem that was apparently of concern to the judicial authorities: how to prevent the drinking of wine by Muslim guests at Christian and Jewish weddings. The simple and obvious solution—to impose the ban on alcohol on everyone—was apparently not considered.

Muslims do not have that degree of independence in their own social and legal life in the modern, secular state. It is no doubt unrealistic for them to expect it, given the nature of the modern state, but that is not how they see it. They feel that they are entitled to receive what they gave. As a Muslim in Europe is said to have remarked, presumably in jest: "We allowed you to practice and even enforce monogamy; why should you not allow us to practice polygamy?"

Such questions—polygamy, in particular—raise important issues of a more practical nature. Isn't an immigrant who is permitted to come to France or Germany entitled to bring his family with him? But what exactly does his family consist of? They are increasingly demanding and getting permission to bring plural wives. The same ruling is also being extended to welfare payments and other benefits.

The contrast in the position of women in the two religiously defined societies has been a sensitive issue, particularly in the age of Muslim defeat and retreat. By defeat in battle, the Muslim was made keenly aware that he had lost his supremacy in the world. By the growth of European control or influence, including the emancipation of his own non-Muslim subjects, he had lost his supremacy in his own country. With the European-inspired emancipation of women, he felt he was in danger of losing his supremacy even in his own house.

The acceptance or rejection of Shari'a rule among Muslims in Europe raises the important question of jurisdiction. In the traditional Sunni juristic view, the Shari'a was part of Muslim sovereignty and jurisdiction and was therefore only applied in the House of Islam, that is to say, in countries under Muslim rule. A minority of the Sunnis and the majority of the Shī'a took the view that the Sharī'a also applied to Muslims outside the House of Islam and should be enforced when possible.

But at no time, until very recently, did any Muslim authority ever suggest that Sharī'a law should be enforced on non-Muslims in non-Muslim countries. The first instance of this new approach was when the Ayatollah Khomeini in Iran pronounced a death sentence for the crime of insulting the Prophet, not only against the Muslim author Salman Rushdi, living in London at that time, but also against all who had been involved in the preparation, production, and distribution of the book—that is to say, the English, presumably non-Muslim editors, printers, publishers, and booksellers. It was followed by an increasing number of other attempts to enforce Sharī'a law in Europe and more recently in other places where Muslims have settled. A notable example was the Muslim response to the famous or infamous Danish cartoons. No less notable were the various European responses to Muslim anger and demand for punishment, ranging from mild reproof to eager acquiescence.

❦

Where does Europe stand now? Is it third time lucky? It is not impossible. The Muslims have certain clear advantages. They have fervor and conviction, which in most Western countries are either weak or lacking. They are for the most part convinced of the rightness of their cause, whereas Westerners spend much of their time in self-denigration and self-abasement. They have loyalty and discipline, and perhaps most important of all they have demography—the combination of natural increase and migration producing major population changes, which could lead within the foreseeable future to significant Muslim majorities in at least some European cities or even countries.

The Syrian philosopher Sādiq al-'Azm has remarked that the remaining question about the future of Europe is this: "Will it be an Islamized Europe, or a Europeanized Islam?" The formulation is a persuasive one, and much will depend on the answer.

But the West also has some advantages, the most important of which are knowledge and freedom. The appeal of genuine modern knowledge in a society that in the more distant past, had a long record of scientific and scholarly achievement is obvious. Present-day Muslims are keenly and painfully aware of their relative backwardness compared with both their own past and their rivals' present, and many would welcome the opportunity to rectify it.

Less obvious but also powerful is the appeal of freedom. In the past, in the Islamic world the word *freedom* was not used in a political sense. Freedom was a legal concept. One was free if one was not a slave. Muslims did not use freedom and slavery as a metaphor for good and bad government, as we have done for a long time in the Western world. The terms they used to denote good and bad government are justice and injustice. A good government is a just government, one in which the holy law, including its limitations on sovereign authority, is strictly enforced. The Islamic tradition, in theory and, until the onset of modernization, to a large degree in practice, emphatically rejects despotic and arbitrary government. The modern style of dictatorship that flourishes in many Muslim countries is an innovation and to a large extent an importation from Europe—first, without any ill intent through the process of modernization, strengthening the central authority and weakening those elements in society that had previously constrained it; second, through the successive phases of Nazi and Soviet influence and example.

Living under justice, in the traditional scale of values, is the nearest approach to what the West would call freedom. But with the spread of European-style dictatorship, the idea of freedom in its Western interpretation is also making headway in the Islamic world. It is becoming better understood, more widely appreciated, and more ardently desired. It is perhaps in the long run our best hope, perhaps even our only hope, of surviving this latest stage—in some respects the most dangerous stage—of a fourteen-century-old struggle.

THIRTEEN

Freedom and Justice in the Modern Middle East

⟨ℛ CHANGING PERCEPTIONS

For Muslims as for others, history is important, but they approach it with a special concern and awareness. The career of the Prophet Muhammad, the creation and expansion of the Islamic community and state, and the formulation and elaboration of the holy law of Islam are events in history, known from historical memory or record and narrated and debated by historians since early times. In the Islamic Middle East, one may still find passionate arguments, even bitter feuds, about events that occurred centuries or sometimes millennia ago—about what happened, its significance, and its current relevance. This historical awareness has acquired new dimensions in the modern period, as Muslims—particularly those in the Middle East—have suffered new experiences that have transformed their vision of themselves and the world and reshaped the language in which they discuss it.

In 1798, the French Revolution arrived in Egypt in the form of a small expeditionary force commanded by a young general called Napoleon Bonaparte. The force invaded, conquered, and excluded, which may be one reason why the British monarchy is still there and the others have gone.

In Middle Eastern monarchies, they never accepted the principle of primogeniture. The general principle in Middle Eastern monarchies was nomination: the ruler nominated his successor-designate. It was not unusual—in fact, it was very frequent—for a sultan to be succeeded by a brother, a nephew, or even a cousin. That has an advantage in that it ensures that the successor is able to take over effectively. It has a disadvantage in that it brings in an element of uncertainty, and we did see a recent example of the sudden, last-minute change in the succession in the Kingdom of Jordan in February 1999. This might have caused trouble, but in fact it didn't. The system held together.

Then we have the tribal monarchies, a term we can apply to Saudi Arabia and most of the Gulf States. These are not monarchies in the sense that Morocco and Jordan are monarchies, but they are quasi-monarchical societies that seem to be holding together for the time being, and in which succession is more or less regulated along monarchical lines. Then there is what we might call a nonhereditary monarchy, and there I refer to Egypt. In Egypt, the monarchy was abolished a long time ago, but we see a remarkable stability and continuity in the Egyptian regime. Nasser died and was succeeded by his deputy Sadat; Sadat was murdered and was succeeded by his deputy Mubarak, and although Mubarak has not nominated a deputy or successor, it seems likely that when he goes the way of all flesh, unless there are radical changes in the meantime, he will be succeeded by someone else from the inner circle. The Egyptians have the advantage of a long-established, smoothly functioning centralized regime that in one sense goes back more than a century, and in another sense, several millennia. Egypt has a political class with considerable experience in keeping control.

We also have what one might call a quasi democracy. I refer, of course, to Iran, where there are contested elections but where a committee decides who may contest the elections, scrutinizes the candidates and may exclude them on a variety of grounds, and controls the results. There are arguments in parliament, and there are arguments in the press; this sometimes leads to unpleasantness for those who put forward the arguments, but there is a modicum of freedom of discussion. There is a certain measure of choice that is a long way short of anything that one could call parliamentary democracy in the Western sense. Until recently, apart from Turkey and Israel, which, as we have seen, were the only two fully functioning democracies in the region, Iran was the country that took third place as the nearest equivalent to a democracy.

And then, of course, we have the one-party state, drawing on fascist and Communist models, which don't really differ very greatly. For a long time, we were all held in the spell of this curious illusion that parliamentary politics—indeed, all politics—can be classified in terms of the seating arrangements of the French National Assembly after the revolution, that is, in terms of left and right. We talk of extreme left and extreme right as if they were at opposite poles; in fact, they are very close to one another, and many were able to make easy transitions from fascist to Communist and from Communist to fascist in central and eastern Europe. The Ba'th Party, branches of which control Syria and until recently controlled Iraq, had its origins in a pro-Nazi group in Vichy-controlled Syria, where, under German auspices, they worked to mobilize support for the pro-Axis Rashīd 'Alī regime in Iraq in 1941. Its origins were largely Nazi-fascist. But as it developed, it became a suitable instrument for the Soviet and quasi-Soviet types of regime that once flourished in Eastern Europe and in some other places, where the party is part of the apparatus of government. But the Ba'th Party was not able to provide for the succession as the Communist Party ruled Egypt without difficulty for several years. General Bonaparte proudly announced that he had come "in the name of the French Republic, founded on the principles of liberty and equality." This was, of course, published in French and also in Arabic translation. Bonaparte brought his Arabic translators with him, a precaution that some later visitors to the region seem to have overlooked.

The reference to equality was no problem: Egyptians, like other Muslims, understood it very well. Equality among believers was a basic principle of Islam from its foundation in the seventh century, in marked contrast to both the caste system of India to the east and the privileged aristocracies of the Christian world to the west. Islam really did insist on equality and achieved a high measure of success in enforcing it. Obviously, the facts of life created inequalities—primarily social and economic, sometimes also ethnic and racial—but these were in defiance of Islamic principles and never reached the levels of the Western world. Three exceptions to the Islamic rule of equality were enshrined in the holy law: the inferiority of slaves, women, and unbelievers. But these exceptions were not so remarkable; for a long time in the United States, in practice if not in principle, only white male Protestants were "born free and equal." The record would seem to indicate that as late as the nineteenth or even the early twentieth century, a poor man of humble origins had a better chance of rising to the top in the Muslim Middle East than anywhere in Christendom, including postrevolutionary France and the United States.

Equality, then, was a well-understood principle, but what about the other word Bonaparte mentioned—"liberty," or freedom? This term caused some puzzlement among the Egyptians. In Arabic usage at that time and for some time after, the word "freedom"—*ḥurriyya*—was in no sense a political term. It was a legal term. One was free if one was not a slave. To be liberated, or freed, meant to be manumitted, and in the Islamic

world, unlike in the Western world, "slavery" and "freedom" were not until recently used as metaphors for bad and good government.

The puzzlement continued until a very remarkable Egyptian scholar found the answer. Sheikh Rifāʻa Rāfiʻ al-Ṭahṭāwī was a professor at the still unmodernized al-Azhar University of the early nineteenth century. The ruler of Egypt had decided it was time to try to catch up with the West, and in 1826 he sent a first mission of forty-four Egyptian students to Paris. Sheikh al-Ṭahṭāwī accompanied them and stayed in Paris until 1831. He was what might be called a chaplain, there to look after the students' spiritual welfare and to see that they did not go astray—no mean task in Paris at that time.

During his stay, he seems to have learned more than any of his wards, and he wrote a truly fascinating book giving his impressions of postrevolutionary France. The book was published in Cairo in Arabic in 1834 and in a Turkish translation in 1839. It remained for decades the only description of a modern European country available to the Middle Eastern Muslim reader. Sheikh al-Ṭahṭāwī devotes a chapter to French government, and in it he mentions how the French kept talking about freedom. He obviously at first shared the general perplexity about what the status of not being a slave had to do with politics. And then he understood and explained. When the French talk about freedom, he says, what they mean is what we Muslims call justice. And that was exactly right. Just as the French, and more generally Westerners, thought of good government and bad government as freedom and slavery, so Muslims conceived of them as justice and injustice. These contrasting perceptions help shed light on the political debate that began in the Muslim world with the 1798 French expedition and that has been going on ever since, in a remarkable variety of forms.

JUSTICE FOR ALL

As Sheikh al-Ṭahṭāwī rightly said, the traditional Islamic ideal of good government is expressed in the term "justice." This is represented by several different words in Arabic and other Islamic languages. The most usual, *'adl,* means "justice according to the law" (with "law" defined as God's law, the Sharī'a, as revealed to the Prophet and to the Muslim community). But what is the converse of justice? What is a regime that does not meet the standards of justice? If a ruler is to qualify as just, as defined in the traditional Islamic system of rules and ideas, he must meet two requirements: he must have acquired power rightfully, and he must exercise it rightfully. In other words, he must be neither a usurper nor a tyrant. It is of course possible to be either one without the other, although the normal experience was to be both at the same time.

The Islamic notion of justice is well documented and goes back to the time of the Prophet. The life of the Prophet Muhammad, as related in his biography and reflected in revelation and tradition, falls into two main phases. In the first phase, he is still living in his native town of Mecca and opposing its regime. He is preaching a new religion, a new doctrine that challenges the pagan oligarchy that rules Mecca. The verses in the Qur'ān, and also relevant passages in the prophetic traditions and biography, dating from the Meccan period, carry a message of opposition—of rebellion, one might even say of revolution, against the existing order.

Then comes the famous migration, the hijra from Mecca to Medina, where Muhammad becomes a wielder, not a victim, of authority. Muhammad, during his lifetime, becomes a head of state and does what heads of state do. He promulgates and enforces laws, he raises taxes, he makes war, he makes peace; in a word, he governs. The political tradition, the political maxims, and the political guidance of this period do not focus on how to

resist or oppose the government, as in the Meccan period, but on how to conduct government. So from the very beginning of Muslim scripture, jurisprudence, and political culture, there have been two distinct traditions: one, dating from the Meccan period, might be called activist; the other, dating from the Medina period, quietist.

The Qur'ān, for example, makes it clear that there is a duty of obedience: "Obey God, obey the Prophet, obey those who hold authority over you." And this is elaborated in a number of sayings attributed to Muhammad. But there are also sayings that put strict limits on the duty of obedience. Two dicta attributed to the Prophet and universally accepted as authentic are indicative. One says, "there is no obedience in sin"; in other words, if the ruler orders something contrary to the divine law, not only is there no duty of obedience but also there is a duty of disobedience. This is more than the right of revolution that appears in Western political thought. It is a duty of revolution, or at least of disobedience and opposition to authority. The other pronouncement, "do not obey a creature against his creator," again clearly limits the authority of the ruler, whatever form of ruler that may be.

These two traditions, the one quietist and the other activist, continue right through the recorded history of Islamic states and Islamic political thought and practice. Muslims have been interested from the very beginning in the problems of politics and government: the acquisition and exercise of power, succession, legitimacy, and—especially relevant here—the limits of authority.

All this is well recorded in a rich and varied literature on politics. There is the theological literature; the legal literature, which could be called the constitutional law of Islam; the practical literature, handbooks written by civil servants for civil servants on how to conduct the day-to-day business of government; and, of course, there is the philosophical literature, which draws heavily on the ancient Greeks, whose work was elaborated in translations and adaptations, creating distinctly Islamic versions of Plato's *Republic* and Aristotle's *Politics*.

In the course of time, the quietist, or authoritarian, trend grew stronger, and it became more difficult to maintain those limitations on the autocracy of the ruler that had been prescribed by holy scripture and holy law. And so the literature places increasing stress on the need for order. A word used very frequently in the discussions is *fitna*, an Arabic term that can be translated as "sedition," "disorder," "disturbance," and even "anarchy" in certain contexts. The point is made again and again, with obvious anguish and urgency: tyranny is better than anarchy. Some writers even go so far as to say that an hour—or even a moment—of anarchy is worse than a hundred years of tyranny. That is one point of view—but not the only one. In some times and places within the Muslim world, it has been dominant; in other times and places, it has been emphatically rejected.

THEORY VERSUS HISTORY

The Islamic tradition insists very strongly on two points concerning the conduct of government by the ruler. One is the need for consultation. This is explicitly recommended in the Qur'ān. It is also mentioned very frequently in the traditions of the Prophet. The converse is despotism; in Arabic *istibdād*, "despotism," is a technical term with very negative connotations. It is regarded as something evil and sinful, and to accuse a ruler of *istibdād* is practically a call to depose him.

With whom should the ruler consult? In practice, with certain established interests in society. In the earliest times, consulting with the tribal chiefs was important, and it remains so in some places—for example, in Saudi Arabia and in parts of Iraq (but less so in urbanized countries such as Egypt or Syria). Rulers also consulted with the countryside's rural gentry, a very powerful group, and with various groups in the city: the bazaar merchants, the scribes (the nonreligious literate classes, mainly civil servants), the religious hierarchy, and the military establishment, including long-established regimental groups such as the Janissaries of the Ottoman Empire. The importance of these groups was, first of all, that they did have real power. They could and sometimes did make trouble for the ruler, even deposing him. Also, the groups' leaders—tribal chiefs, country notables, religious leaders, heads of guilds, or commanders of the armed forces—were not nominated by the ruler, but came from within the groups.

Consultation is a central part of the traditional Islamic order, but it is not the only element that can check the ruler's authority. The traditional system of Islamic government is both consensual and contractual. The manuals of holy law generally assert that the new caliph—the head of the Islamic community and state—is to be "chosen." The Arabic term used is sometimes translated as "elected," but it does not connote a general or even sectional election. Rather, it refers to a small group of suitable, competent people choosing the ruler's successor. In principle, hereditary succession is rejected by the juristic tradition. Yet in practice, succession was always hereditary, except when broken by insurrection or civil war; it was—and in most places still is—common for a ruler, royal or otherwise, to designate his successor.

But the element of consent is still important. In theory, at times even in practice, the ruler's power—both gaining it and maintaining it—depends on the consent of the ruled.

Some critics may point out that regardless of theory, in reality a pattern of arbitrary, tyrannical, despotic government marks the entire Middle East and other parts of the Islamic world. Some go further, saying, "That is how Muslims are, that is how Muslims have always been, and there is nothing the West can do about it." That is a misreading of history. One has to look back a little way to see how Middle Eastern government arrived at its current state.

The change took place in two phases. Phase one began with Bonaparte's incursion and continued through the nineteenth and twentieth centuries, when Middle Eastern rulers, painfully aware of the need to catch up with the modern world, tried to modernize their societies, beginning with their governments. These transformations were mostly carried out not by imperialist rulers, who tended to be cautiously conservative, but by local rulers—the sultans of Turkey, the pashas and khedives of Egypt, the shahs of Persia—with the best of intentions but with disastrous results.

Modernizing meant introducing Western systems of communication, warfare, and rule, inevitably including the tools of domination and repression. The authority of the state vastly increased with the adoption of instruments of control, surveillance, and enforcement far beyond the capabilities of earlier leaders, so that by the end of the twentieth century, any tin-pot ruler of a petty state or even of a quasi state had vastly greater powers than were ever enjoyed by the mighty caliphs and sultans of the past.

But perhaps an even worse result of modernization was the abrogation of the intermediate powers in society—the landed gentry, the city merchants, the tribal chiefs, and others—which in the traditional order had effectively limited the authority of the state. These intermediate powers were gradually weakened and mostly eliminated, so that on the one hand the state was getting stronger and more pervasive, and on the other hand the limitations and controls were being whittled away.

The second stage of political upheaval in the Middle East can be dated with precision. In 1940, the government of France surrendered to Nazi Germany. A new collaborationist government was formed and established in a watering place called Vichy, and General Charles de Gaulle moved to London and set up a Free French committee. The French empire was beyond the reach of the Germans at that point, and the governors of the French colonies and dependencies were free to decide: they could stay with Vichy or rally to de Gaulle. Vichy was the choice of most of them, and in particular the rulers of the French-mandated territory of Syria-Lebanon, in the heart of the Arab East. This meant that Syria-Lebanon was wide open to the Nazis, who moved in and made it the main base of their propaganda and activity in the Arab world.

It was at that time that the ideological foundations of what later became the Ba'th Party were laid, with the adaptation of Nazi ideas and methods to the Middle Eastern situation. The nascent party's ideology emphasized pan-Arabism, nationalism, and a form of socialism. The party was not officially founded until April 1947, but memoirs of the time and other sources show that the Nazi interlude is where it began. From Syria, the Germans and the proto-Ba'athists also set up a pro-Nazi regime in Iraq, led by the famous, and notorious, Rashīd 'Alī al-Gailānī.

The Rashīd 'Alī regime in Iraq was overthrown by the British after a brief military campaign in May–June 1941. Rashīd 'Alī went to Berlin, where he spent the rest of the war as Hitler's guest with his friend the mufti of Jerusalem, Haj Amin al-Husseini. British and Free French forces then moved into Syria, transferring it to Gaullist control. In the years that followed the end of World War II, the British and the French departed, and after a brief interval, the Soviets moved in.

The leaders of the Ba'th Party easily switched from the Nazi model to the Communist model, needing only minor adjustments. This was a party not in the Western sense of an organization built to win elections and votes. It was a party in the Nazi and Communist sense, part of the government apparatus particularly concerned with indoctrination, surveillance, and repression. The Ba'th Party in Syria and the separate Ba'th Party in Iraq continued to function along these lines.

Since 1940 and again after the arrival of the Soviets, the Middle East has basically imported European models of rule: fascist, Nazi, and Communist. But to speak of dictatorship as being the immemorial way of doing things in that part of the world is simply untrue. It shows ignorance of the Arab past, contempt for the Arab present, and unconcern for the Arab future. The type of regime that was maintained by Saddam Hussein—and that continues to be maintained by some other rulers in the Muslim world—is modern, indeed recent, and very alien to the foundations of Islamic civilization. There are older rules and traditions on which the peoples of the Middle East can build.

CHUTES AND LADDERS

There are, of course, several obvious hindrances to the development of democratic institutions in the Middle East. The first and most obvious is the pattern of autocratic and despotic rule currently embedded there. Such rule is alien, with no roots in either the classical Arab or the Islamic past, but it is by now a couple of centuries old and is well entrenched, constituting a serious obstacle.

Another, more traditional hurdle is the absence in classical Islamic political thought and practice of the notion of citizenship, in the sense of being a free and participating member of a civic entity. This notion, with roots going back to the Greek *polites*, a member of the *polis*, has been central in Western civilization from antiquity to the present day. It, and the idea of the people participating not just in the choice of a ruler but in the conduct of government, is not part of traditional Islam. In the great days of the caliphate, there were mighty, flourishing cities, but they had no formal status as such, nor anything that one might recognize as civic government. Towns consisted of agglomerations of neighborhoods, which in themselves constituted an important focus of identity and loyalty. Often, these neighborhoods were based on ethnic, tribal, religious, sectarian, or even occupational allegiances. To this day, there is no word in Arabic corresponding to "citizen." The word normally used on passports and other documents is *muwāṭin*, the literal meaning of which is "compatriot." With a lack of citizenship went a lack of civic representation. Although different social groups did choose their own leaders during the classical period, the concept of choosing individuals to represent the citizenry in a corporate body or assembly was alien to Muslims' experience and practice.

Yet, other positive elements of Islamic history and thought could help in the development of democracy. Notably, the idea of consensual, contractual, and limited government is again becoming an issue today. The traditional rejection of despotism, of *istibdād*, has gained a new force and a new urgency: Europe may have disseminated the ideology of dictatorship, but it also spread a corresponding ideology of popular revolt against dictatorship.

The rejection of despotism, familiar in both traditional and, increasingly, modern writings, is already having a powerful impact. Muslims are again raising—and in some cases practicing—the related idea of consultation. For the pious, these developments are based on holy law and tradition, with an impressive series of precedents in the Islamic past. One sees this revival particularly in Afghanistan, whose people underwent rather less modernization and are therefore finding it easier to resurrect the better traditions of the past, notably consultation by the government with various entrenched interests and loyalty groups. This is the purpose of the Loya Jirga, the "grand council" that consists of a wide range of different groups—ethnic, tribal, religious, regional, professional, and others. There are signs of a tentative movement toward inclusiveness in the Middle East as well.

There are also other positive influences at work, sometimes in surprising forms. Perhaps the single most important development is the adoption of modern communications. The printing press and the newspaper, the telegraph, the radio, and the television have all transformed the Middle East. Initially, communications technology was an instrument of tyranny, giving the state an effective new weapon for propaganda and control.

But this trend could not last indefinitely. More recently, particularly with the rise of the Internet, television satellites, and cell phones, communications technology has begun to have the opposite effect. It is becoming increasingly clear that one of the main reasons for the collapse of the Soviet Union was the information revolution. The old Soviet system depended in large measure on control of the production, distribution, and exchange of information and ideas; as modern communications developed, this became no longer possible. The information revolution posed the same dilemma for the Soviet Union as the Industrial Revolution did for the Ottoman and other Islamic empires: either accept it and cease to exist in the same manner or reject it and fall increasingly behind the rest of the world. The Soviets tried and failed to resolve this dilemma, and the Russians are still struggling with the consequences.

A parallel process is already beginning in the Islamic countries of the Middle East. Even some of the intensely and unscrupulously propagandist television programs that now infest the airwaves contribute to this process, indirectly and unintentionally, by offering a diversity of lies that arouse suspicion and questioning. Television also brings to the peoples of the Middle East a previously unknown spectacle—that of lively and vigorous public disagreement and debate. In some places, young people even watch Israeli television. In addition to seeing well-known Israeli public figures "banging the table and screaming at each other" (as one Arab viewer described it with wonderment), they sometimes see even Israeli Arabs arguing in the Knesset, denouncing Israeli ministers and policies—on Israeli television. The spectacle of a lively, vibrant, rowdy democracy at work, notably the unfamiliar sight of unconstrained, uninhibited, but orderly argument between conflicting ideas and interests, is having an impact.

Modern communications have also had another effect, in making Middle Eastern Muslims more painfully aware of how badly things have gone wrong. In the past, they were not really conscious of the differences between their world and the rest. They did not realize how far they were falling behind not only the advanced West but also the advancing East—first Japan, then China, India, South Korea, and Southeast Asia—and practically everywhere else in terms of standard of living, achievement, and, more generally, human and cultural development. Even more painful than these differences are the disparities between groups of people in the Middle East itself.

Right now, the question of democracy is more pertinent to Iraq than perhaps to any other Middle Eastern country. In addition to the general factors, Iraq may benefit from two characteristics specific to its circumstances. One relates to infrastructure and education. Of all the countries profiting from oil revenues in the past decades, pre-Saddam Iraq probably made the best use of its revenues. Its leaders developed the country's roads, bridges, and utilities, and particularly a network of schools and universities of a higher standard than in most other places in the region. These, like everything else in Iraq, were devastated by Saddam's rule. But even in the worst of conditions, an educated middle class will somehow contrive to educate its children, and the results of this can be seen in the Iraqi people today.

The other advantage is the position of women, which is far better than in most places in the Islamic world. They do not enjoy greater rights—"rights" being a word without meaning in that context—but rather access and opportunity. Under Saddam's predecessors, women had access to education, including higher education, and therefore to careers, with few parallels in the Muslim world. In the West, women's relative freedom has been a major reason for the advance of the greater society; women would certainly be an important, indeed essential, part of a democratic future in the Middle East.

FUNDAMENTAL DANGERS

The main threat to the development of democracy in Iraq and ultimately in other Arab and Muslim countries lies not in any inherent social quality or characteristic, but in the very determined efforts that are being made to ensure democracy's failure. The opponents of democracy in the Muslim world come from very different sources, with sharply contrasting ideologies. An alliance of expediency exists between different groups with divergent interests.

One such group combines the two interests most immediately affected by the inroads of democracy—the tyranny of Saddam in Iraq and other endangered tyrannies in the region—and, pursuing these parallel concerns, is attempting to restore the former and preserve the latter. In this the group also enjoys some at least tacit support from outside forces—governmental, commercial, ideological, and other—in Europe, Asia, and elsewhere, with a practical or emotional interest in its success.

Most dangerous are the so-called Islamic fundamentalists, those for whom democracy is part of the greater evil emanating from the West, whether in the old-fashioned form of imperial domination or in the more modern form of cultural penetration. Satan, in the Qur'ān, is "the insidious tempter who whispers in men's hearts." The modernizers, with their appeal to women and more generally to the young, are seen to strike at the very heart of the Islamic order—the state, the schoolroom, the market, and even the family. The fundamentalists view the Westerners and their dupes and disciples, the Westernizers, as not only impeding the predestined advance of Islam to final triumph in the world, but even endangering it in its homelands. Unlike reformers, fundamentalists perceive the problem of the Muslim world to be not insufficient modernization, but an excess of modernization—and even modernization itself. For them, democracy is an alien and infidel intrusion, part of the larger and more pernicious influence of the Great Satan and his cohorts.

The fundamentalist response to Western rule and still more to Western social and cultural influence has been gathering force for a long time. It has found expression in an increasingly influential literature and in a series of activist movements, the most notable of which is the Muslim Brotherhood, founded in Egypt in 1928. Political Islam first became a major international factor with the Iranian Revolution of 1979. The word *revolution* has been much misused in the Middle East and has served to designate and justify almost any violent transfer of power at the top. But what happened in Iran was a genuine revolution, a major change with a very significant ideological challenge, a shift in the basis of society that had an immense impact on the whole Islamic world, intellectually, morally, and politically.

The theocratic regime in Iran swept to power on a wave of popular support nourished by resentment against the old regime, its policies, and its associations. Since then, the regime has become increasingly unpopular as the ruling mullahs have shown themselves to be just as corrupt and oppressive as the ruling cliques in other countries in the region. There are many indications in Iran of a rising tide of discontent. Some seek radical change in the form of a return to the past; others, by far the larger number, place their hopes in the coming of true democracy. The rulers of Iran are thus very apprehensive of democratic change in Iraq, the more so as a majority of Iraqis are Shi'ites, like the Iranians. By its mere existence, a Shi'ite democracy on Iran's western frontier would pose a challenge, indeed a mortal threat to the regime of the mullahs, so they are doing what they can to prevent or deflect it.

Of far greater importance at the present are the Sunni fundamentalists. An important element in the Sunni holy war is the rise and spread—and in some areas dominance—of Wahhabism. Wahhabism is a school of Islam that arose in Nejd, in central

Arabia, in the eighteenth century. It caused some trouble to the rulers of the Muslim world at the time but was eventually repressed and contained. It reappeared in the twentieth century and acquired new importance when the House of Saud, the local tribal chiefs committed to Wahhabism, conquered the holy cities of Mecca and Medina and created the Saudi monarchy.

The first great triumph of the Sunni fundamentalists was the collapse of the Soviet Union, which they saw—not unreasonably—as their victory. For them the Soviet Union was defeated not in the Cold War waged by the West, but in the Islamic jihad waged by the guerrilla fighters in Afghanistan. As Osama bin Ladin and his cohorts have put it, they destroyed one of the two last great infidel superpowers—the more difficult and the more dangerous of the two. Dealing with the pampered and degenerate Americans would, so they believed, be much easier. American actions and discourse have at times weakened and at times strengthened this belief.

In a genuinely free election, fundamentalists would have several substantial advantages over moderates and reformers. One is that they speak a language familiar to Muslims. Democratic parties promote an ideology and use a terminology mostly strange to the "Muslim street." The fundamentalist parties, on the other hand, employ familiar words and evoke familiar values both to criticize the existing secularist, authoritarian order and to offer an alternative. To broadcast this message, the fundamentalists utilize an enormously effective network that meets and communicates in the mosque and speaks from the pulpit. None of the secular parties has access to anything comparable. Religious revolutionaries, and even terrorists, also gain support because of their frequently genuine efforts to alleviate the suffering of the common people. This concern often stands in marked contrast with the callous and greedy unconcern of the current wielders of power and influence in the Middle East. The example of the Iranian Revolution would seem to indicate that once in power these religious militants are no better, and are sometimes even worse, than those they overthrow and replace. But until then, both the current perceptions and the future hopes of the people can work in their favor.

Finally, perhaps most important of all, democratic parties are ideologically bound to allow fundamentalists freedom of action. The fundamentalists suffer from no such disability; on the contrary, it is their mission when in power to suppress sedition and unbelief.

Despite these difficulties, there are signs of hope, notably the Iraqi general election in January. Millions of Iraqis went to polling stations, stood in line, and cast their votes, knowing that they were risking their lives at every moment of the process. It was a truly momentous achievement, and its impact can already be seen in neighboring Arab and other countries. Arab democracy has won a battle, not a war, and still faces many dangers, both from ruthless and resolute enemies and from hesitant and unreliable friends. But it was a major battle, and the Iraqi election may prove a turning point in Middle Eastern history no less important than the arrival of General Bonaparte and the French Revolution in Egypt more than two centuries ago.

FEAR ITSELF

The creation of a democratic political and social order in Iraq or elsewhere in the Middle East will not be easy. But it is possible, and there are increasing signs that it has already begun. At the present time there are two fears concerning the possibility of establishing a democracy in Iraq. One is the fear that it will not work, a fear expressed by many in the United States and one that is almost a dogma in Europe; the other fear, much more urgent in ruling circles in the Middle East, is that it will work. Clearly, a genuinely free society in Iraq would constitute a mortal threat to many of the governments of the region, including both Washington's enemies and some of those seen as Washington's allies.

The end of World War II opened the way for democracy in the former Axis powers. The end of the Cold War brought a measure of freedom and a movement toward democracy in much of the former Soviet domains. With steadfastness and patience, it may now be possible at last to bring both justice and freedom to the long-tormented peoples of the Middle East.